PUBLISHED BY BOOM BOOKS

www.boombooks.biz

ABOUT THIS SERIES

.... But after that, I realised that I knew very little about these parents of mine. They had been born about the start of the Twentieth Century, and they died in 1970 and 1980. For their last 20 years, I was old enough to speak with a bit of sense.

I could have talked to them a lot about their lives. I could have found out about the times they lived in. But I did not. I know almost nothing about them really. Their courtship? Working in the pits? The Lock-out in the Depression? Losing their second child? Being dusted as a miner? The shootings at Rothbury? My uncles killed in the War? Love on the dole? There were hundreds, thousands of questions that I would now like to ask them. But, alas, I can't. It's too late.

Thus, prompted by my guilt, I resolved to write these books. They describe happenings that affected people, real people. The whole series is, to coin a modern phrase, designed to push your buttons, to make you remember and wonder at things forgotten. The books might just let nostalgia see the light of day, so that oldies and youngies will talk about the past and re-discover a heritage otherwise forgotten. Hopefully, they will spark discussions between generations, and foster the asking and answering of questions that should not remain unanswered.

BORN IN 1954?
WHAT ELSE HAPPENED?

RON WILLIAMS

AUSTRALIAN SOCIAL HISTORY

BOOK 16 IN A SERIES OF 35

FROM 1939 to 1973

War Babies Years (1939 to 1945): 7 Titles

Baby Boom Years (1946 to 1960): 15 Titles

Post Boom Years (1961 to 1973): 13 Titles

BOOM, BOOM BABY, BOOM

BORN IN 1954? WHAT ELSE HAPPENED?

Published by Boom Books.
Wickham, NSW, Australia
Web: www.boombooks.biz
Email: jen@boombooks.biz

© **Ron Williams 2013. This edition 2023**

Creator: Williams, Ron, 1934 - author
Title: Born in 1954? : what else happened? / Ron Williams.
ISBN: 9780994601544
Australia--History--Miscellanea--20th century.

Cover images: National Archives of Australia

A1773, RV1339, Queen's visit;

A6201,62, Mrs Petrov;

A12111, 1/1954/21/1, mowing the yard,

A1200, L18540, Redex trial.

CONTENTS

IMPORTANT PEOPLE AND EVENTS

Queen of England	Elizabeth II
Prime Minister of Oz	Robert Menzies
Leader of Opposition	Doc Evatt
The Pope	Pope Pius XII
PM of Britain	Winston Churchill
US President	Dwight Eisenhower

Winner of the Ashes:

1953	England 1 - 0
1954-5	England 3 - 1
1956	England 2 - 1

Melbourne Cup Winners

1953	Wodalla
1954	Rising Fast
1955	Toparoa

Sydney to Hobart

1953	Solvig
1954	Kurrewa IV
1955	Even

INTRODUCTION

This book is the sixteenth in a series of books that I aim to publish. It tells a story about a number of important or newsworthy events that happened in 1954. The series will cover each of the years from 1939 to 1973, for a total of 35 books, which should just about bring me to the end of my thoroughly undistinguished writing career.

I developed my interest in writing these books a few years ago at a time when my children entered their teens. My own teens began in 1947, and I started trying to remember what had happened to me then. I thought of the big events first, like Saturday afternoon at the pictures, and cricket in the back yard, and the wonderful fun of going to Maitland on the train for school each day. Then I recalled some of the not-so-good things. I was an altar boy, and that meant three or four Masses a week. I might have thought I loved God at that stage, but I really hated his Masses. And the schoolboy bullies, like Greg Farrell, and the hapless Freddie Evans. Yet, to compensate for these, there was always the beautiful, black headed, blue-sailor-suited June Brown, who I was allowed to worship from a distance.

I also thought about my parents. Most of the major events that I lived through came to mind readily. But after that, I realised that I really knew very little about these parents of mine. They had been born about the start of the Twentieth Century, and they died in 1970 and 1980. For their last 20 years, I was old enough to speak with a bit of sense. I could have talked to them a lot about their lives. I could have found out about the times they lived in. But I did not. I know almost nothing about them really. Their courtship?

Working in the pits? The Lock-out in the Depression? Losing their second child? Being dusted as a miner? The shootings at Rothbury? My uncles killed in the War? There were hundreds, thousands of questions that I would now like to ask them. But, alas, I can't. It's too late.

Thus, prompted by my guilt, I resolved to write these books. They describe happenings that affected people, real people. In **1954,** there is some coverage of international affairs, but a lot more on social events within Australia. This book, and the whole series is, to coin a modern phrase, designed to push the reader's buttons, to make you remember and wonder at things forgotten. The books might just let nostalgia see the light of day, so that oldies and youngies will talk about the past and re-discover a heritage otherwise forgotten. Hopefully, they will spark discussions between generations, and foster the asking and the answering of questions that should not remain unanswered.

The sources of my material. I was born in 1934, so that I can remember well a great deal of what went on around me from 1946 onwards. But of course, the bulk of this book's material came from research. That meant that I spent many hours in front of a computer reading electronic versions of newspapers, magazines, Hansard, Ministers' Press releases and the like. My task was to sift out, **day-by-day**, those stories and events that would be of interest to the most readers. Then I supplemented these with materials from books, broadcasts, memoirs, biographies, government reports and statistics. And I talked to old-timers, one-on-one, and in organised groups, and to Baby Boomers about their recollections. People with stories to tell come out of the woodwork, and talk no end about the tragic and funny and commonplace events that have shaped their lives.

The presentation of each book. For each year covered, the end result is a collection of short Chapters on many of the topics that concerned ordinary people in that year. I think I have covered most of the major issues that people then were interested in. On the other hand, in some cases I have dwelt a little on minor frivolous matters, perhaps to the detriment of more sober considerations. Still, in the long run, this makes the book more readable, and hopefully it will convey adequately the spirit of the times.

Each of the books is mainly Sydney based, but I have been deliberately national in outlook, so that readers elsewhere will feel comfortable that I am talking about matters that affected them personally. After all, housing shortages and strikes and a tuberculosis epidemic involved **all** Australians, and other issues, such as problems overseas, had no State component in them. **Overall, I expect I can make you wonder, remember, rage and giggle equally, no matter where you hail from.**

SOME POLITICS FROM 1953

Australian politicians, both in the Federal sphere and in the States, had a good start to 1954. The previous year had ended without any major controversies hanging over them, the nation's economy was in pretty good shape, most people were employed and indulging regularly in the national hobby of striking at will. Electricity supplies were almost adequate but still provided ample opportunity for grumbling, so generally the nation was happy enough.

New houses were slowly but surely reducing the housing shortage emanating from the War and the Baby Boom, electric lawn mowers were affordable, and Hire Purchase was available over and above the elusive first-mortgage bank loan. Sunday afternoons were spent at the family barbie, and Monday nights were reserved for working out how much longer the house mortgage would be on the books. The answer always seemed to be over twenty years, at this stage.

All of this left our politicians quite contented. Of course, they were **always** open to criticism, and **as always**, they were worthy of it. Their performance in their various Legislative Chambers was childish and destructive of good government, day after day. They were generally juvenile in their conduct, were always running round snapping at the heels of their opposition, seemed incapable of even understanding a straight question, and had no idea of creating policies other than some cheap give-aways to vocal pressure groups.

At the Federal level, the Liberal Party was currently in power, and many readers will know that they remained in power for about another 14 years. The one strong **electoral** platform they could always rely on when pressed was their anti-Communist ideology. Their crafty and intelligent Leader, Bob Menzies, was always ready to use the so-called Red menace to whip the Labor Party back onto the Opposition benches.

Communism at the time in Australia had two faces. The first, the international one, was constantly forced into our gaze by our American friends, who spent much of their energy trying to prove that their Capitalist system was superior in every way to the Communism of the USSR. We in Australia were awash with the propaganda that this effort generated, and part of Menzies' bag of tricks was to frighten us, every day if possible, with the potential terrors of the Red scourge.

The other face of Communism in Australia that was visible was in our Trade Unions. Many, in fact most, of our Unions were controlled by Communists. This was **not**, in general, because the workers were in favour of international Communism, but rather because the local Reds were well organised, and prepared to go out on a limb against the perceived vices of the local bosses. These activists thought that the strike weapon was the right one to use, and so the nation was always plagued by tons of impromptu strikes. Menzies was annoyed by these strikes, but that did not stop him from exploiting them. He could condemn them to the full as damaging our national economy, and at the same time he could point out that this was part of the Red strategy to conquer the world by internal subversion.

The Labor Party was poorly placed to answer Menzies' charges. **Firstly**, they were unconvincingly led by Doc Evatt and Arthur Calwell, neither of whom was noted for his moderation or stability. **Second**, the Labor Party had many within its ranks who still clung to the Socialist ideology that included far greater State control of the population than most people wanted. This brought the Labor Party dangerously close to the ideas of some Communists and it was always open to charges that it was in bed with the Communists. **Third**, the Trade Unions were part and parcel of the Labor Party, and given that these Unions were controlled by the Reds, it was easy to believe that there were all sorts of links to and fro.

In all, Labor was battling uphill to hold its own in the Oz electorate, and it was **little wonder**, in retrospect, that they **did stay in the political wilderness** for so long after 1954.

Then their position was always worse because the Labor Party drew its electoral support from the workers, who in turn were unionised, and that meant that the Party always had to defer to the Reds in the unions. The mud-slingers had many field days.

The Liberals were in the happy position of having plenty of mud, and the mud-slinger par excellence, Prime Minister Bob Menzies. He had been pushing the anti-Red barrow for over a decade, and every time he raised the Red herring, he scared people with the prospect of a revolution. **Probably by now he knew that the Reds were no threat to the nation** at all, but there was no way he would admit this.

This is the background to politics throughout this book. I won't harp on it, but I ask you to occasionally remember that the big difference between the Parties was their attitude to Communism.

THE PLACE OF THE MONARCHY

King George VI died in 1952. His daughter, Princess Elizabeth, was crowned Queen in the middle of 1953. At the beginning of 1954, she and Prince Phillip had cruised their way through the islands of the Pacific, and were currently in New Zealand, just about ready to re-plant the British flag in Australia.

Her coronation had been a huge success. All the pomp and spangle you would expect, executed with the best of British reserve, it was seen as a symbol of the solidarity of the British Empire, and of the resurrected might of Britain. Within Australia, millions of ordinary people had been thrilled by the grand spectacles, and completely won over by the beauty and grace of their new Queen.

And right now, this new sovereign was about to land in Australia. There was a small, but growing, number of people who were questioning our allegiance to Britain. Most of these had become disillusioned during the War when Churchill refused to co-operate with Oz Prime Minister Curtin by providing the support to Australia that Britain had always promised. At the time, there were a lot of questions asked about the value of an alliance that seemed to work to the benefit of only one party - Britain. But, with the arrival of the Queen, such discontent was directed towards the British Government, and not to the monarchy, nor to the monarch herself.

So it seems that Australia was all ready for one big party in a few weeks. Already the preparations had been going on for months. Politicians and their wives had been jockeying for invitations to functions, and had been arguing over how much money they should be paid for the time they spent at such parties. Some of the grey moss had been cleaned off the Sydney Harbour Bridge, and flags and commemorative bits of junk had been placed everywhere. People had argued in the Press that their own bit of heaven should be graced by a Royal visit despite, in one case, the lack of public toilets in their historic town.

On top of that we were told that the visit was excellent for "the economy". Tons of money would be spent, and that would have a stimulatory effect. A few cynics said that all that would happen would be that **existing** cash would flow from the working classes to the merchants and the Government, and that no **new wealth** would be created. But, these were just a bunch of party-poopers and few people would listen amidst all the excitement.

So, my readers, get yourself ready for the glamour and glitz of **the Royal Tour of 1954**. You will not see another like it.

THE INTERNATIONAL SCENE

Two major themes were apparent. **The first** was the ongoing battle between the goodies and the baddies, also known as Communism and Capitalism. Or the other way round if you like. Whatever you decide, the Russians and the Americans were locked in a 40-year battle of ideologies, where each of them said that **it was better in all respects than its opposite number**, and if a war broke out, it could belt the living daylights out of its opponent. But, each of them also contended, **it** was benign and friendly and charitable to all and sundry, and any nation would be wise to align fully with it.

Australia was firmly in the American camp as far as foreign policy was concerned. We were ourselves quite committed to the capitalist philosophy, and in practice were happy enough to follow America's lead in international affairs. But the urgency and frenetic worry that marked such matters in the US was absent in Oz. Here, we could simply sit back and watch with interest as the Chinese built up their forces near South East Asia. And here we could take with a yawn the news that the goodies and baddies were once again nearly coming to blows over the occupation of West Berlin. It all seemed too remote to worry about, and who would be mad enough to actually start fighting over such disputes?

The second theme was seen in the efforts of dozens and dozens of small nations to get free of their colonial masters. During the War, the passion for independence among these nations had grown, and in the post-war era almost every one of them was at some stage or other in its fight to control its own destiny. Whether it was the black nations of Africa, or the hundreds of former Dutch islands of Indonesia, or the great British Dominion of India, every one of them wanted to be freed from their former British, Dutch and French masters.

This meant that the news was full, day after day, of reports of incidents between the dominant white rich exploiters (or developers, if you like) and the poor oppressed native populations of dozens of nations. In fact, most often, the colonial powers were coming to accept that it was time to move out, but inevitably the transfer of power was taking too long, so that violence on the ground was common.

In Australia, once again, we could watch with interest. Such unrest was a long way from our shores. We did have our own problems with Aborigines in Oz. And we had potential difficulties with the natives in New Guinea. But neither of these races was militant at the moment, and so once again Australia remained a nice comfortable haven from which to observe the world.

1954 – HERE WE COME

So now we are just about ready to plunge into 1954. But first, one little diversion. I give you below a few Rules that I use in writing this series. That will help you to understand where I am coming from.

MY RULES IN WRITING

NOTE. Throughout this book, I rely a lot on **reproducing Letters from the newspapers**. Whenever I do this, I put the text in a different font, and indent it a little, and make the font somewhat smaller. I do not edit the text at all. That is, **I do not correct spelling or grammar**. If the text gets at all garbled, I do not correct it. It's just as it was seen in the Papers.

SECOND NOTE. The material for this book, when it comes from newspapers, is reported as it was seen at the time. If the benefit of hindsight over the years changes things, then I might record that in my Comments. The information reported thus reflects matters as they were seen in 1954.

THIRD NOTE. Let me also apologise in advance to anyone I might offend. In a work such as this, it is certain some people will think I got some things wrong. I am sure that I did, but please remember, all of this is only my opinion. And really, my opinion does not matter one little bit in the scheme of things. **I hope you will say "silly old bugger"**, and shrug your shoulders and read on.

JANUARY NEWS ITEMS

What a start to the New Year. Australia had been down 2-1 versus America in the **Davis Cup tennis**. On New Year's Day, **we came back to win 3-2**....

Lew Hoad and Ken Rosewall were the new Oz heroes. Rosewall was only 18 years old. Nearly every radio set in the nation spent three days **listening to a ball-by-ball description of the action**. **Tennis was now the great national passion.**

The Queen's New Year's Honours list included Patti Menzies, the wife of Prime Minister Robert. It is expected that the Queen will add further to her list when she concludes her visit to Australia soon.

Australian newspapers were obsessed, in the first week of January, by **the Queen in New Zealand**. Her visit to a glow-worm cave, and to various waterfalls were prominent. In the meantime, Bondi Beach and its surrounds were being sharpened up. For example, **the bulb over the small pool will be replaced**.

Fourteen major American tobacco companies announced last night that they had established a fund to investigate **whether** smoking was somehow linked to cancer. A spokesman said that smoking was being blamed for almost every ailment, and it was time to provide convincing evidence that **it did not impact cancer. Remember their aim is to disprove the link.** I would expect that if a positive link is found, then the results will not be published. That is the way, then and now, that science often works.

On January 28th, it was announced that the **Pope had a continuous bout of hiccups**. This left him slightly indisposed, and he had to cancel a general audience for 12,000 people due that day.

The *Sydney Morning Herald* (*SMH*) started a campaign against those police who were accused of accepting bribes and turning a **blind eye to organised gambling in Sydney**. All major Oz cities had illegal two-up schools, and **their whereabouts were well known to everyone.** Including, of course, the police. The *Herald* was trying to make this into Big News.

The US has proposed that a big naval survey of the Pacific Islands be undertaken, under its command. **It proposes to use some Japanese surveyors.** Popular opposition in Australia has risen to such an extent that Australia is considering what actions it **might** take to prevent their use. **The War is still not forgotten in Oz.**

David Rogers, of Balgowlah, wrote passionately that judges at Sydney's 86th Annual Highland Gathering had indicated that **kilts should just touch the ground when kneeling**. They said,"In general, the kilt is being worn too short." He claims that this is the wrong standard, and that kilts should be clearly above the top of the knee-cap.

That would make them about **three inches shorter than what the judges suggested**. He claims that the "touch the ground" dictum had been argued for fifty years, but had now gone into the discard.

PRELUDE TO THE QUEEN

January is usually a slack month in Australia. Most of the nation takes a three week break from work, school holidays last for the entire month, and many people take a holiday and rent a house or go camping on the coast. For a writer like myself, there are only a few big stories, as journalists also take their holidays, and **the bad news from overseas is not printed** by the newspapers because Editors know that January is not the month for it. It is a time of put your feet up, have a cup of tea or a beer, or maybe a swim, watch the cricket or tennis, and vow that this year you will not get caught once more into the rat-race.

Right now, the papers were full of gripping stories. A girl in England, heiress to the fortunes of an Italian magnate, had eloped with a young farmhand to Scotland. The father threatened to disown her, but relented. The young man had to cut his honeymoon short because his sick father needed him to milk the cows. This story was spread over seven days, and you can see just how gripping it was.

Then there was the story of an unheard-of British Duchess who was most distressed because she lost ten places in the British rankings for the Nation's Best Dressed Women. She realised that her down-grading was because she had kept her skirts at a length two inches below the knees, whereas others had raised theirs three inches. She was refusing to lift her skirts any further, "despite the consequences."

Papers carried lots of news from America. Most of it was propaganda in their Cold War against Russia. But other more cultural matters did get a bit of space. For example, during January we were told that US singer, Johnny Ray, got a divorce. Also that Marilyn Monroe had been married a second time, to baseballer Joe Dinajio, also a second-timer. The American columnist reporting this quipped that "Marilyn can't catch a ball, but she has never missed a baseballer." Oh dear.

At the same time, cultural figures Jane Russell and Gina Lollobrigida complained that Hollywood studios were focusing movie-goers' attention on their bodies, and they were not getting a chance to display their true artistic talents.

LETTERS IN JANUARY

People on holidays - in January - write to the newspapers about topics that are different from other times of the year. **By February**, Letter-writers are serious, very earnest, writing to denounce wrongs, or to persuade others to do something they consider worthy. Or perhaps to criticise Governments, or politicians, or taxes. **In January, however**, Letters were often deliberately frivolous, or half-full of nonsense, with no real barrow to push. I have given two of these below, and you will see what I mean.

Letters, A Howe. The housewife who complained recently that a snail was served with her salad has not lived in the near Orient, where snails served with salad, add to the cost of the dish.

Oysters are sea snails, and no one objects to oysters, with or without salad, either raw or cooked. The ordinary garden snail is a most fastidious clean feeder, and three well-grown garden snails would equal in vitamin-content one fresh egg. Well-cooked snails, with shells removed, furnish quite an attractive garnish to a Chinese curry, and look like oysters of a small size.

Chinese chefs, also those in Malaya and Japan, fold the snail into a semicircular form if without shell. If cooked in its shell the snail is well boiled and removed carefully.

A ring of prawns and a ring of snails make an attractive setting for small lobsters served in their red cases on lettuce or chopped cabbage – a colourful dish for a cocktail lunch.

Letters, John A McCallum. An announcement was made recently by the Minister for Transport that all double decker buses would be replaced by single decker buses.

This announcement and the absence of any public discussion since it was made, is a striking instance of bureaucratic tyranny and public apathy. The reason for the change may be completely convincing to the mind of the person concerned solely with moving the greatest number of people in the shortest possible time, and yet completely unsatisfactory from the point of view of men, women and children who travel.

It is possible that the greatest number of those who travel by buses prefer double deckers to single deckers. Evidence for this is the fact that many people always sit on the top deck if possible. London continues to use double decker buses and they appear to move people as expeditiously and more comfortably than the single decker buses of New York and Paris.

Will the Minister, at least, give the people of Sydney an opportunity of expressing their opinions on this matter?

WOOL AND WHEAT

Australia's two biggest sources of overseas income in 1954 were wool and wheat, both of which were sold in large quantities to Britain. Early in the 1950's, prices for these commodities rose sharply, as the war in Korea got under way. Since then, prices had come down a bit, but they were still good money-earners for the nation.

A problem was on the horizon for wheat, though. We had been   producing a lot of it, and perhaps we had quite a surplus building up. Adequate storage facilities to stockpile wheat had not been built during the War, and so people were starting to ask what we should do with the immediate surplus. Some were starting to realise that we **could** sell to markets outside of Britain, but such thinking was in its infancy.

One prominent official had a suggestion that stirred some holiday commentators into writing. Sir John Teasdale, Chairman of the Australian Wheat Board, suggested that it was now time **that we reduce production of wheat across the nation, and thus avoid future surpluses.**

Not surprisingly, not everyone agreed. A host of writers said that it was a most astounding statement, coming as it did from **the head of a marketing board.** His job, they argued, was to find new markets, and expand the scope for exports. Some went on to argue that he should be calling for increased production and expanding our selling points. A few others said that he and his Board were the cause of the problem, because all they wanted to do was ship wheat out to Britain, and had played no part in raising **the quality** of our wheat. Now that the entire world was past the post-

War famine stage, it was calling out for higher protein wheat, and we could not provide it. The existing Board had done nothing to meet this situation.

Sir John Teasdale was by now having a bad month. But other Letter-writers had some more to say.

Letters, Rev G H Officer. The suggestion by various clergymen on Sunday last that Australia's surplus wheat should be used "to feed the starving millions of South-East Asia," does not take into consideration two practical problems of primary importance. **One.** The staple food of these people is rice. Would they, therefore, be able to use wheat if they did receive it?

Two. Who is to pay for it. The people for whom it is intended obviously cannot, and the producer should not be expect to do so. "The Government" – as some might suggest – has no authority to spend taxpayers' money on such a scheme.

Admittedly the needs of South-East Asia are great, but it is to be regretted that proposals for the relief of this need should be notable more for their emotional appeal than for their realism.

Letters, Rev H M Arrowsmith, St Andrew's Cathedral, Sydney. The amount of food wasted in Australia today is scandalous and almost a crime against humanity. Can we add to that culpability **the further sin of limiting food production** at a time when our near-neighbour countries are starving?

Some generalities may be misleading, and I do not want to fall into that error. But it is probably true that tonight one half of the world's population will go to bed hungry.

How far can the Christian conscience of this country break through the economic and fiscal tyranny which dictates a refusal to produce. If Australia today should fail to grow and to distribute the maximum food she can produce, then as a nation we deserve the judgment of God that we are unworthy of our heritage and callous in the face of the need of our Asiatic neighbours.

Letters, Poultry Farmer. I have nothing against the proposal to make available some of our surplus wheat to the world's underfed peoples at a price they can pay, or even as has been suggested, giving it to them.

But why not first let our own poultry industry benefit from cheaper wheat, and so benefit the whole community by lowering the price of eggs.

The Housewives' Association claims that eggs are too dear, and suggests a boycott of one of the most valuable and necessary foods known. This futile and defeatist policy would be on a par with **the wickedly selfish proposal to reduce our wheat production**. Do the housewives know that many poultry-farmers are making only a bare living and that they lost thousands of laying hens in the recent heatwave? Also that at present prices of wheat, bran and pollard, many poultry-farmers are fed up and seriously inclined to "give the game away?" Does the Housewives' Association want to put this valuable industry out of business altogether?

When drought, flood, fire, or other disaster strikes at the farmer or grazier, a paternal Government hastens to afford some relief, but the poultry-farmer bears his losses and battles on unaided. Of course eggs are too dear, and it all comes back to the exorbitant price demanded for wheat.

Comment. Prime Minister Menzies brought all discussion to an end when, mid-month, he said emphatically that **there would be no limits set on production of wheat** for the nation. He pointed out, sensibly, that a world glut in wheat can change almost overnight when crops on various continents fail. He went on to say that our aim is to produce wheat, and then to sell it. We needed to break the habit of always relying on Britain's markets, and instead find new ones elsewhere.

THE QUEEN IS ALMOST HERE

By the end of January, Elizabeth and Phillip had almost finished their extensive tour of New Zealand, and a few days later would be ready for their visit to the real centre of the universe. As January progressed, the flurry caused by the impending tour grew and grew, until by the end of the month it was almost stifling. Mind you, it was not all froth and bubble.

For example, it had **already been decided** that the City of Sydney would display 1,200 large flags at points in the City that the Queen would visit. Also, that the NSW Cabinet, made up of 16 Members, must wear full formal dress, including Hombergs, at receptions. The hostesses for the royal plane had been chosen, and their smiling faces were beaming from all newspapers in Oz. Note that there no male flight attendants at the time.

Of course, Letters were starting to pour in. The very first ones were all about transport and the like.

Letters, Lloyd Ross, acting Secretary, Australian Railways Union. Preparations for the Royal visit have been associated with serious argument on precedence, with discussion on behaviour and dress, as well as with less seemly scrambles for invitations to Royal functions. These indicate how important the event is considered to be.

The demand that seniority be followed in **selecting a guard for the Royal train** should be regarded in the same level of importance. To those who are directly concerned, it is no more trivial than the order to be followed in being presented to her Majesty. Seniority to railway workers is as vital as the order of precedence to a Parliamentarian. The guard who mans her Majesty's train will feel honoured and his prestige raised; it may be regarded as one of the most outstanding experiences in his career.

Our critics are inconsistent. At one moment they are claiming that the issue is so trivial as to be merely a storm in a "railway teacup"; in another moment, they claim that the occasion is so special that the Commissioner should have untrammeled rights to select the train crew.

We take the view that the occasion is such an important one, that seniority should be respected – unless questions of ability are raised – which are not, in fact, involved in this case.

Nothing was more serious than the various routes the Queen should travel. Letters were requesting and demanding that such and such a town or suburb should be honoured. The Letters below are typical.

Letters, L D Evans. I notice that the Tour Authorities will not agree to a deviation of route to allow the Queen, on her trip to Newcastle, to join the train at Hornsby instead of Central station. This deviation should not affect the time schedule. A car trip from Government House to Hornsby would take no longer than a car to Central and the train to Hornsby.

The North Shore, from Chatswood onwards, is the most attractive part of Sydney, and a great number of people will be given a chance to see the Queen and of expressing their loyalty to the Royals.

It has been mentioned that this deviation would enable crippled children from Strathallen and Margaret Reid Hospitals to have their only chance of seeing the Royal party. In addition to these youngsters, there are **the polio children**, who have a home on Pacific Highway. Many thousands of schoolchildren would also be given a sight they would never forget.

I doubt whether there is a better 20 miles of road surface in Sydney, or a better 20 miles' drive as far as trees, footpaths, homes and general cleanliness and freshness than in the upper North Shore.

The Royal tour authorities would be well advised to reconsider their decision and give some consideration to a quarter of a million people, and also, I am sure, make the trip to Newcastle more pleasant for the Queen.

Letters, R Thomas. The suggestion that the Queen travel to Newcastle by car is a dangerous one. If it were necessary to stop for a bathroom break, there are only a few garages that provide facilities, and these are always in disgusting condition. Also, the lavatory seats always have a host of red-back spiders under them and nearby. Hardly fit for a Queen.

Letters, B H Goldsworthy. I cannot agree with those who seem to think that the Queen's city progress on February 3 should not take her through some of the poorer streets of Sydney.

Her Majesty is no stranger to mean streets. Shortly after her Coronation, she and the Duke made a tour of the East End of London. Obviously she wishes to see and be seen by all her people; and if some might find it impossible to come to the more prosperous areas, then she will graciously come to them.

Letters, W Siddens, Rector, St Thomas', North Sydney. Many citizens of North Sydney are disappointed by the rejection of requests that on one of the occasions when the Queen visits North Sydney, she should be given the opportunity of passing the splendid and historic church of St Thomas.

This would enable the Queen to witness the place where her grandfather, King George V, and his brother, the Duke of Clarence, stood when they set the foundation-stone of the Baptistry. The spacious and sloping grounds surrounding the Church would provide a vantage point for at least 3,000 spectators.

These early Letters were followed by bagfuls of bright suggestions covering every possible aspect of the tour. I present a small sample below, and you will notice that some of them are sensible.

Letters, J F. I was shocked to read that prominent **Communists** may be invited to attend functions in the Queen's honour in Sydney.

As these persons are opposed to all that the Queen represents – the Throne and the Church – this must be abhorrent to every worthy and patriotic member of the community. It is to be hoped that those directing such a great event as the Royal visit will act resolutely and see that it is not marred.

Letters, Mary Knight. Why have no tickets been issued to the men who were on Gallipoli and their wives to see the Queen when she lands at Farm Cove, drives through the city streets, or reviews of troops in Hyde Park? Totally incapacitated soldiers and their attendants rightly have tickets for seats in Hyde Park.

But many of the men who made the name Anzac, and are now getting old and fewer, are incapable of standing for a long time. These are the men who helped make

Australia great and the name Anzac revered throughout the world.

If politicians and their wives receive three and four tickets, surely some could be spared for these men.

Letters, J Blumer. During the Royal visit could not some attention be given to deportment?

One cannot help noticing the slovenly manner in which the National Anthem is received. I suggest that at least the men stand to attention when the anthem is played or sung.

Letters, Alan Campbell. I read that the Royal car on February 3 will be flanked by mounted police.

Even at 6 mph, it is going to be difficult for the ordinary man in the street to catch a glimpse of her Majesty, let alone try to see her through a screen of prancing horses. In all the newsreels we have seen of the Royal processions in Fiji, Tonga and New Zealand, no such screen has been drawn over our Sovereign. In her homeland, where crowds twice the size of any in Australia gather, no mounted police cordon is ever thrown around the car.

Everyone acknowledges the splendid bearing of the NSW mounted police, but seeing the Queen is the reason that large crowds will be lining the streets.

Letters, Clive Goodwin, St Mark's Rectory, Darling Point. Is the Federal Government sincere in its desire to encourage the people to decorate worthily for the Royal visit?

If so, why is it charging 12½ per cent sales-tax on motifs that will only be of use on this occasion and then stacked away or destroyed? It is reasonable to assume that they will take many hundreds of thousands of pounds from the taxpayers in this way.

Letters, Ruth Bedford. I wonder if those in charge of the Queen's visit to Sydney have arranged for **cheer leaders** to be stationed at intervals along the streets?

I have never yet heard a Sydney crowd cheer – not even when their men return from war. They are strangely self-conscious, and the Queen will not understand a silent crowd. She is used to enthusiastic cheers wherever she goes. I fancy this strange silence is due to our great processions on Anzac day, a day when cheers are not suitable. But this is a time of rejoicing, and the Queen should be so greeted as to leave no doubt of our welcome.

Letters, M Forster. I have read the suggestion that our Queen would appreciate eating a cake made with one or more **emu eggs**. Might I point out that emus are protected birds in NSW, and that to be found in possession of its egg – or portion of an egg, or its shell for that matter – is an offence.

Over the past 30 years I have watched the emu disappear from huge areas of the north and north-west. This has been brought about mainly by the nests being disturbed and the eggs stolen by people who were too lazy to keep a few domestic fowls. It is to be hoped that no misguided individual will attempt to make a cake from an emu egg at this time of the year. Emus seldom lay after November, and do not commence again before April at the earliest.

FEBRUARY NEWS ITEMS

In America, **the infamous Senator Joe McCarthy was** continuing his anti-Communist campaign through his Senate Committee for UnAmerican Activities. For a year he had been a scourge of people like Hollywood actors, and now **he was wanting to pass laws that automatically found all members of the Communist Party guilty of treason**. They were then to be imprisoned....

Cooler heads prevailed, and **such legislation was never passed**. Joe McCarthy was so successful in his persecutions because there were so many Americans who were almost **hysterically opposed to Communism**. It was all part of the Cold War.

Athletic types are getting excited about the prospect of the **running of a 4-minute mile**. **John Landy**, an Australian, is the great white hope. **My own forecast: No one will ever do it.**

February 11th. **John Landy will make an attempt on the record** at tonight's Athletics meeting at the Sydney Cricket Ground. **Prince Phillip** hopes to attend to watch. When the Royal train gets in to Sydney from Wollongong, **he will be rushed to the Ground to see the mile-event**, whose start will be delayed as long as possible for him.

Race result: Landy managed a time of 4 minutes and six seconds, in windy conditions. The Duke did get there half an hour late, and was cheered when he made his appearance.

The New Zealand Prime Minister offered the world some advice on behaviour during the Queen's visit. *Be natural* when you talk to the Queen. *Stand six feet* from the Royal Car as it passes to get a better view of the Queen. *Gather in groups in country towns* so that Royal progress can slow down for a better view, and people are not strung out.

Back in Oz, an official reminder was made by **Tour officials** that the Royal couple would shake hands with hundred of persons. Persons so honoured should therefore shake hands in **the lightest possible manner**.

Letter-writer Tom Burke of Gosford commented "If I can get within 50 yards of the entourage as it sweeps by, **I will certainly remember the good advice.**"

The Royal visit to Canberra in a few days faces many hurdles. One is with the cadets at the Royal Military College at Duntroon. The Queen is to present new colours to a corp of cadets, and **that will involve a religious blessing. Catholic cadets**, 40 of them, are prevented by Church rules from **attending non-Catholic services. Will cooler heads prevail? Yes, they did. Cardinal Mannix saids that it was OK to attend.**

Fourteen aldermen at Katoomba have surrendered their right to **shake hands with the Queen** at a civic welcome. They unanimously decided that they forego the pleasure so that the Queen would have more time to view **the splendour of the Blue Mountains.**

THE QUEEN STEPS ASHORE

On February 3rd, Queen Elizabeth and her husband, Prince Phillip, planted foot on Australia, at Sydney. They were met by 1 million cheering citizens, who had somehow come to the city over the last twenty fours hours, and who were standing six deep along every route that the Royal couple would traverse. After disembarking from the brand-spanking new Royal yacht *Britannia*, the pair were ensconced in Government House, and straight away started on their whirlwind of public engagements.

Over the next week, among other events, they opened State Parliament, banqueted several times with high dignitaries, attended the Lord Mayor's Ball, graced a luncheon for women groups at the Trocadero, and attended church at St Andrew's Cathedral. All the while, huge crowds followed their every move, and cheered on the right occasions, and peered into the distance to catch a glimpse of the Queen as she passed by.

A daytime event at the Sydney Town Hall won the record for faintings. Over 2,000 women in the crowd fainted and needed attention. Other venues daily had good fainting scores, but this figure was clearly the best.

Sydney did not keep the Queen just to itself. After a few days, she went by Royal train to Newcastle, where she was shown over the local beauty spots, including the BHP steelworks. Then off by plane to Lismore. Back to Sydney that night. Off to Wollongong next day, and that was the day the Duke arrived back in time for the John Landy attack on the four-minute mile.

After a few days, off she went to Bathurst, and Dubbo and other inland cities. Then down to Canberra, where she opened the Australian Parliament's next sitting. That night, she enjoyed a "family dinner" with 800 guests. Two nights later, she honoured "the most brilliant Ball in Australia's history" with her presence. This ball was celebrated by 500 Oz celebrities from all walks of life. The ABC band, led by Jim Gussey, played firstly a waltz, and then sambas, rhumbas, quicksteps and a Windsor waltz. Albert Namatjira was there. He commented that it was "good tucker." Papua New Guinea representative Willie Gavera commented that "We could buy a wife with all those pigs."

It was a wonderful night, but sadly it signalled the beginning of the end for NSW. A few days later, the Queen and Phillip, back in Sydney, boarded the *Britannia* and slowly edged their way through the flotilla of craft that had assembled as a guard of honour. On the dock behind them, they left "scores" of weeping women, and some men, who were bereft at the Royal departure. On board, however, they went off on their merry way towards Tasmania where, it seemed, their welcome would be as tumultuous as in Sydney.

Still, not everyone was sad to see them go. About 30 prisoners were released from Long Bay Gaol in time to see the Queen depart. They were the first batch to benefit from the remission of sentence – by Royal prerogative – because of the Queen's visit.

NEWS AND VIEWS OF THE NSW TOUR

Letters, D. Finer details of courtesy and hospitality have been absent at some points of the Royal itinerary.

By whose mismanagement was it that her Majesty was not immediately taken to a rest room and provided with cool drinks at Concord Repatriation Hospital, without having herself to ask for a drink of water after her arduous drive in the heat?

Again, by whose thoughtlessness was her Majesty left without the shade of a suitably canopy at the Bondi surf carnival? Surely officials who organised the carnival did not think one umbrella sufficient to provide enough shade?

Letters, A R Loton, Royal Tour Surf Carnival Committee. It is evident that "D" was not present at the Royal surf carnival at Bondi.

A canopy was provided by the organising committee at considerable expense, ready for unfurling at a minute's notice. However, with a pleasant ocean breeze and a sun which had lost its sting by 3.30, it was not the desire of her Majesty that this be done, as it was her wish, as at all times, that she see and be seen by as many of her subjects as possible.

Letters, (Mrs) Elizabeth Daly. Can we not see more young people at the functions attended by the Queen?

Up to the present, her Majesty has been surrounded by a great majority of people old enough to be her parents.

Letters, G A King. Many citizens, adults as well as children, dearly love trains, and I suggest to Mr Winsor that after the Royal tour of New South Wales has concluded, the railway carriage used by the Queen and the Duke of Edinburgh should be open for inspection for a small fee. The proceeds of the inspection might be donated to a selected charitable fund, preferably one within the Railways Department.

Letters, (the Rev) Ralph Ogden, Milson's Point. "God Save the Queen" is surely Australia's true and proper National Anthem. It clearly refers to Australia's own Queen and national sovereignty, and also to the spiritual and Royal links uniting the world-wide Commonwealth.

Embarrassments such as Column Eight mentions show that a great majority have never accepted "Advance Australia" as a substitute or joint anthem and now see less reason than ever for doing so. Why, indeed, stand up to baldly boast about ourselves and our God-given natural resources, in words which mention neither God nor our Queen?

Letters, Anglican Campanologist. The sound of bells was not heard when the Queen attended St Andrew's Cathedral in Sydney. The day her Majesty arrived three churches on the route of the Royal progress were ringing peals – St Mary's Cathedral, St Benedict's, Broadway, and Christ Church St Laurence – but no bells were heard at St Andrew's.

When the Queen visits Hobart, the St David's Cathedral bells will ring out the changes in the old English style, and bells will also ring when she visits St Paul's, Melbourne, and St Peter's, Adelaide, also St George's Cathedral, Perth.

Is there not money that can be used to provide St Andrew's with the voices of bells.

I am reminded, too, that in the case of the proposed Memorial Carillon at Canberra, no provision has been made to have some of the bells for change-ringing in the English style.

In England today there are 5,226 peals of bells compared with nine carillons. Why cannot Australia keep up the change-ringing tradition by hanging perhaps 10 or 13 of these carillon bells for the art that is maintained by more than 40,000 persons in England.

Letters,   Catholic   Campanologist.   "Anglican Campanologist's" letter is correct in almost every detail, but a slight addition would add further interest.

In my practical experience over the last 54 years, St Mary's Cathedral, St Mark's, Darling Point, Christ Church St Laurence and All Saints', Parramatta, have taken part in ringing both muffled and open in honour of all Royal and distinguished visitors and at the death of all members of the Royal family.

My first official ring was the welcome to the then Duke of York, later to become King George V. I rang for the opening of the first National parliament of Australia, an event in which all churches with peals of bells combined to take part – St Mary's, Christ Church St Launce, St Philip's, Church Hill, St Mark's, Darling Point, St Jude's, Randwick, and All Saints', Parramatta.

In all those years it has had me puzzled why St Andrew's Anglican Cathedral has not at least one peal of bells. I have often inspected the twin towers (from the outside) which could accommodate two peals. I have questioned some of my Anglican friends and the only reason from those friends is lack of finance. Why?

On the day of the Royal progress, the bells of St Benedict's, Broadway, were rung in part or wholly, so I understand, by the Anglican ringers of All Saints', Parramatta. These good ladies and gentlemen filled the bill as St Mary's Cathedral ringers could not supply an extra team.

CHILDREN IN HOSPITALS

In all this jubilation, there was at least one, more serious, topic for public discussion.

Letters, Future Rebel Parent. Ignorance is seldom an excuse for cruelty and never where the victim is a child. I refer to the cold insistence of hospitals on **severing all contact between a sick child and his parents except one visiting day a week.**

In Melbourne's Royal Children's Hospital, parents visit twice daily and assist in the ward care of their youngsters. When parents are unable to visit, kindergarten teachers act as mother-substitutes. In visit-starved children's hospitals and children's wards **in Sydney,** many parents accept a hospital sister's statement that their presence upsets the child. These even forgo the Sunday visit, little realising just how much the distressed child needs the constant daily reassurance and comfort of his parents' presence.

Letters, (Mrs) Bodah Quinn. I agree with "Rebel Parent", who exposed the harsh rule of the children's hospitals in allowing only two hours a week visiting time for sick children in public wards. Who is responsible for this archaic rule, blindly adhering to a system that was out of date years ago in England and America?

For the timid and nervous child, the period in hospital in a public ward must be a time of emotional stress, causing more harm than the condition from which he is suffering.

In the private section of the hospital, visitors enjoy the privilege of visiting twice a day every day in the week, so the statement of the hospital sister that the presence of parents upsets the child is obviously nonsense.

Hospital superintendents and staffs pride themselves on the physical care they give children in the pubic wards, but they are entirely oblivious of the mental stress they cause both to child and parents by allowing only two hours a week visiting time.

Letters, 'Another Rebel Mother', Orange. We recently had the same heart-rending experience as "Rebel Parent", with our child in the public ward of a hospital. We had prepared him for his stay in hospital, and he was quite happy to go, but when he found mum and dad had deserted for a whole week at a time his heart and his spirit were broken.

Sunday visitations were something to be dreaded, not looked forward to, as he would hold on to us tightly and beg us not to leave. On many occasions he asked if we could come every day.

Our boy went to the hospital a happy, normal, lovable child, but when he came home his confidence in us was sadly lacking. It has taken plenty of care and love to restore him to his normal happy nature, and he continually asks our reassurance that he will not be sent back to hospital.

Next time, it will be to a private ward, where we will at least be near him each day, even if it means a big sacrifice. I would advise any mother with a preschool-age child to send the child only to a private ward until these out-of-date rules and regulations are revised.

Letters, Enid Bell. Passing through the children's section of a suburban hospital one dismal Sunday afternoon, I saw a child of about two and a half years crying in his cot. There was no one in the ward except another sleeping baby. The half-drawn blinds, the strangers passing along the corridor, the absence of anything faintly resembling home and familiar surroundings, must have had anything but a healing effect.

If the child in question was well enough to pad up and down his small cot, chewing fretfully at the wooden railing, he was well enough to be nursed and comforted by his or her mother. When visiting hours were over, and I passed the ward on my way home, the little one was still crying miserably.

Comment. Hospital matrons in 1954 generally had a reputation for being terrifying. They ran their nurses and sisters and patients with a rod of iron, and imposed a strict, no-nonsense discipline on all staff. While Letters on the subject poured in for two weeks, they chose not to reply, despite the fact that the issue was clearly in their policy domain. No one was surprised at this, because it was typical of their I-don't-answer-to-anyone attitude.

Looking back now, from 2016, it seems hard to believe that so many people, including parents, accepted such a system. As I work my way through this book, I will doubtless say a number of times that "some things never change". Fortunately, I can't say that here.

NEWS AND VIEWS

At various stages in this book, I will pull together a few odd items, mainly Letters. Some are a bit silly, others more serious that illustrate some of the quirky things that kept people busy.

Letters, (Mrs) Edith Clarke. Because of the recent rains after the drought there are hundreds of mushrooms to be had here for the picking.

We have bottled over 2,000 according to instructions by the expert, Fowler, but have found by past experience they do not keep for more than six weeks.

Could any country woman advise us on this matter, as the Labor involved is wasted for such a short period.

I did think of adding 1 tablespoon of brandy to each bottle, but before doing so I would like to hear the opinions of others.

Letters, A W. Mrs Clarke who has asked how to bottle mushrooms so that they will keep well, may not know that a good way is to dry the mushrooms in an oven.

When all the moisture has evaporated, they can be stored in bottles and require only to be soaked in warm water for an hour before cooking. I learned this from the famous French chef, Chateney.

Letters, J B. I have on my pantry shelf a number of mushrooms bottled in 1950 and still wholesome.

I washed the mushrooms, packed them in small jars with sufficient salt, clipped on the lid over the rubber, then placed the jars 3 at a time in a large pressure cooker for 20 minutes after it reached cooking heat. I did not add water before cooking. When done the mushrooms occupied only about a quarter of the jar.

Letters, Puzzled, Yowie Bay. While it seems to be generally acknowledged that going out to work is good for mothers, it would be interesting to know what arrangements working mothers make during school holidays.

Are there really thousands of employers who let their employees "down tools" intermittently to fit in with school holidays and infectious diseases? What happens to the child when it is off-colour with a severe cold or a bilious attack?

These are questions which confront me when I myself contemplate the pleasure of adding to my inadequate housekeeping money and breaking up the monotony of household chores.

Letters, D Ashken.   May I, as a "working mother," suggest to "Puzzled" that she makes her inadequate housekeeping money go round for as long as possible before taking a job.

No one who is not a mother can fully appreciate the harm which is done to children, especially young ones, when their mother goes out to work. The strain involved on young children in getting themselves off to school, letting themselves into an empty house with their own key, and spending the day or days alone in bed when they are indisposed is considerably.

In a society where ever-rising prices make it a stark necessity in some cases for the mother to augment the family income, she would be wise to cut her hours of work down to the absolute minimum which will produce the necessary extra income.

MARCH NEWS ITEMS

A rare sound was heard on the Royal Tour: Booing. When the Queen arrived at Melbourne Town Hall for a ceremony, mounted police took up positions between the crowd and Her Majesty. Several hundred people who had waited in the front row for hours could no longer see, and responded in accordance with tradition.

The Government announced that the estimated total cost for the Snowy River Scheme would be $422 million, rather that the original estimate of $442m. This is remarkable. **It is almost unheard of for costs of major projects to fall.** Mind you, the final cost came in at much more than these estimates, so there was ultimately a reversion back to normality.

Four Puerto Ricans, led by a 34-year old woman, **fired 34 bullets into the public vestibule of the US Congress** today. Three Congressmen were lightly wounded, with similar damage to four spectators. **The Ricans were protesting against American imperialism.**

A portrait of Prime Minister Menzies was found with a two-foot slash in it. It was hung in King's Hall Parliament House, along with that of all previous Prime Ministers and Speakers of the Houses. Experts have been called in to see if it can be repaired.

A full-scale **atomic-powered** electricity generation plant will be built in the US over the next few years.

In Sydney, six men dived to a depth of 112 feet by so-called **"skin-diving".** **They had gas tanks strapped to**

their backs. This depth is believed to be an Australian record, though no official figure is kept.

On Sunday, **in Melbourne**, three divers went to a depth of 117 feet, wearing units that had been invented by one of the men. It pumps oxygen into the lungs. He (Edward Eldred) **holds the world patent for the device**. It will enable swimmers to stay under water for an hour.

At last, **the UK is protesting against nuclear testing by the US in the Pacific.** After several H-bomb tests that damaged natives and fishermen in the vast region, upcoming tests are being viewed with concern in the UK and elsewhere. **"The Pacific is not an American lake"** and "The decision to risk widespread contamination is not for the US alone."

The English Grand National **Steeplechase** at Aintree was won yesterday by Irish horse Royal Tan. The race was not without incident. **Four of the 29 starters died during it**, and only nine finished. The winning jockey, Bryan Marshall, has been racing for 24 years, and has broken almost every bone in his body.

Port Pirie, in South Australia, is being asked to consider a proposal for **milk to be delivered in plastic containers** so that it can be **thrown over the fence** like a newspaper.

People with nothing to do were counting the **number of uses of the word "master"** in current jargon. Usage varies from "headmaster" to "mixmaster". To date the official total is 64.

WILL PUBS STAY OPEN AFTER SIX?

The battle lines were being drawn again. A new hours-of-closing controversy was on the cards. A large part of the population of NSW wanted the current disgusting conditions for drinking in hotels to be changed somehow to make them more acceptable. They were suggesting that extending the closing time for pubs from 6pm until some later time would allow this.

Another part of the population said that there was already too much drinking in the State, and that no such extension should be allowed. Some of these people, often of religious background, went on to say that no drinking at all should be possible. The balance between the two groups was not known at the moment, but a learned Judge, Maxwell, had just pronounced that **a referendum** should be conducted so as to resolve the matter. In the other States, similar moves were afoot at the same time.

No specific proposals had yet been put forward for the ballot. Still, Letters from interested parties flowed in.

Letters, George Foote. People in general cannot visualise a proposed new condition; they, therefore, cling to the old familiar one, whether it be good or deplorable.

Reform is the task of the leaders, not of the people; if the reform called for by the Maxwell Report is to be decided by referendum, it will never be carried out.

Letters, A Manefield, NSW Methodist Conference. Mr Robson should have sought the guidance of his friends before he attempted his smear campaign against churchmen who advocate retention of 6 o'clock closing for hotels.

Had he done so he would have learned that the unholy alliance he mentions is a figment of its own imagination and the expression of superficial reasoning.

Churchmen stand by 6 o'clock closing for reasons of their own, and are not in alliance with any liquor interest. We flatly oppose any undemocratic attempt to alter trading hours without the vote of the people to do so.

Letters, J Cochrane, Retired Police Sergeant. All hotels licensed to sell intoxicating liquors are public places and should never be closed; by keeping them open there would be no overcrowding in bars and less drinking, and it would help stamp out sly-grog selling.

Letters, Belle Carlin. One tiny question: Who is to look after the children in the home whilst mother and father participate in this nocturnal conviviality?

Are they to be left to their own devices, or should a baby-sitter be called in?

Letters, A Hemmons. In view of all the conditions peculiar to Australia, and to NSW in particular, the only way to change the inborn habits of the people will be to encourage more drinking in the home, and less in the pubs.

Changing the hours will make no appreciable difference when so many people are ready to swill beer at any hour if a pub is open. To break this habit down, far more bottled beer will be wanted. Brewers, whether they like it or not, will have to undertake a lot more bottle washing. Beer bottles could carry a charge to ensure return, and then there would be fewer bottles lying about.

Instead of more fully licensed houses, the English "off licence" shop should be encouraged. This establishment (no "tied house") would deal in bottle or draft beer, not to be drunk on the premises. Breweries would be required to deliver orders in crates, and take back empties.

Letters, Adrian B Walker. As one who has lived in London and on the Continent, I would say that the average Australian drinker is not one who should be trusted with the freedom of extended drinking hours as enjoyed by those overseas.

In London one may see the benefit of late closing. Husbands and wives and members of their families congregate at night in the homely and pleasant atmosphere of hotels. They are seated at tables, or, in lower-class areas, on forms around the bars, and enjoy each other's company and conversation, also food and perhaps music, and they drink moderately.

In Paris again we see sane drinking.

Could, or would, Australians adapt themselves to this innocuous form of enjoyment? I think not. They are for the greater part essentially guzzlers and will probably always remain so. Perhaps they are born so, perhaps the climate has something to do with it. Whatever the cause, however, it would seem wise to walk warily before granting them greater latitude.

Letters, K Smith. The community tends to regard the drunk with misplaced tolerance – to be mollified if abusive, humoured if a nuisance, and assisted if helpless. But if they were treated as the disgusting, usually objectionable, and frequently dirty, intemperate creatures they are, and the laws against public nuisance applied, drunkenness would become an unpopular and expensive pastime, and then decent, well-behaved citizens would use alcohol as the mild, refreshing and frequently beneficial stimulant it is.

Letters, W Ashley-Brown (Archdeacon), formerly Dean of Gibraltar, Chatswood. The beer swill seems due to several causes. Over his beer when work is done, the ex-Serviceman rightly enjoys the old comradeship. But he has not been taught how to drink like a civilised Christian and guzzles his beer. Owing to the prevalent high wages, he has money to spare and thrift is not necessary. Owing to the identification of official Protestantism with extreme Puritanism, the religion of the majority has never faced the duty of teaching its young how one of God's good gifts may be enjoyed in temperance and sobriety, and that its abuse, but not its use, is a grave sin like theft or immorality.

During 20 years' service in India, I knew very few total abstainers, but intemperance was as rare. The same applied in Aden, the Persian Gulf, and Gibraltar. In Spanish villages, friends met in the local fonda and chatted for an hour or so over a glass of light wine costing a couple of pence.

Letters, Let's Grow Up. Churchmen, temperance societies, and others would have one believe that later trading hours would disrupt the family life. On the contrary, I think we have ample proof that it is 6 o'clock closing that is disrupting family life.

Many married couples have no children, many married people have grown-up families, and many adults of both sexes are unmarried. Are all these responsible individuals to be deprived of the pleasure of an occasional evening in a hotel lounge because of the extremely doubtful hypothesis that those with young families would neglect them for the same purpose? Surely not.

Frankly, I am somewhat envious of my husband going into the hotel at 5 o'clock with his men friends. Usually at that time, I am at home preparing the evening meal, and this makes it difficult for me to join him. My husband and I have agreed it would be much nicer if we could now and again go to the local hotel for a few drinks after dinner, as we did when we lived in America and England. Without exception, all our married and unmarried friends hold the same view. What's wrong with that?

Comment. The breweries owned almost all the pubs. They had been great assets for half a century, but I will specify **two things** that were changing this. **The first** was the growth of the licensed club movement, such as the RSLs, golf and bowling clubs and League clubs. These were springing up everywhere, and were selling beer in decent surroundings, with meals, and entertainment. They were soon to undercut the profits of the pubs.

The second was that the pubs themselves were getting old and bedraggled. They were good enough to drink beer in if you could stand pig-swill conditions, but not if you wanted anything better. For example, people were now asking for decent accommodation from pubs. Even if the hoteliers wanted to provide this, most of them could not because their premises were too run down. The costs of fixing them up were great indeed, and once again there was a new competitor. **The new idea of motels** was starting to spread across America, and would soon make a big impact in Australia. These were of a reasonable standard, and the beat-up old pubs could not compete.

So while this battle over the referendum was happening over the next few years, stronger underlying forces were white-anting the breweries' position, and at the same time, providing some services that civilised people should expect. Not that it happened overnight. **It took years, in fact decades,** before decent drinking and eating and accommodation conditions spread across the nation.

THE QUEEN IS STILL TOURING

From the end of February, the Royal Party moved from one State to the next, generally spending two or three days in the capital, and a couple visiting the hinterland. After she left Sydney, the Queen had a restful two day cruise to Tasmania, where her reception was just as enthusiastic as it had been in Sydney.

By the time she got to Melbourne, the Queen felt like having another Ball. Melbourne agreed. It was the biggest and most lavish Ball of the tour.

Newspapers reported it as below.

The official guest list allowed for 6,000, but fully 8,000 magnificently gowned women and immaculately clad men jammed the floor of the huge barn-like ballroom. No City Council official would explain why there were more guests present than anticipated, but obviously there had been some "trading" in tickets.

The Queen and Duke of Edinburgh did not arrive until 9.30, but guests began to assemble before 7 o'clock. They had a long and dry vigil, for although the capacious bars groaned with 100 nine-gallon kegs of beer and many hundreds of bottles of spirits, no drinks were served until the Royal Party entered.

Only a few "fanatics" attempted to dance while the Queen was present because nobody could hear the orchestra above the din as thousands milled around the Royal box to catch a glimpse of Her Majesty. As the Queen and Duke entered the Royal box there was the greatest pushing and shoving exhibition yet seen on the tour. Dowagers stood with the others on chairs to see the Royal couple. The staring was blatant.

Huge banks of massed flowers, a stage back-drop depicting Windsor Castle, and brilliant lighting transformed the huge barn-like building. Glassed Boar's heads and masses of red, white, and blue gladioli set in ice were the principal decorations.

By 10 o'clock the floor was littered with cigarette butts, pieces of damp moss from the flower beds, and bits of tulle torn from skirts. Nobody showed any inclination to dance even after the Lord Mayor had presented 23 Councillors and their wives to the Queen and the Duke.

The Queen wore a crinoline frock of frosty white tulle and Vandykes of gold thread at the waistline. She wore the Order of the Garter, the Royal Family orders, a superb diamond tiara, and a diamond and emerald necklace.

Forty security men were on duty in and around the building, and a guard was at every door. The guards were augmented by dozens of firemen, because the old wooden building is a notorious fire risk.

Most of the guests had a modest supper. They were blue or pink ticket-holders. They were served a running buffet meal of cold meats, fish, with salad and standard trifles, ice cream, fruit salad and somewhat smaller raspberries. These guests had coffee but no intoxicants with their supper.

AFTER THE BALL WAS OVER

After that grand feast, the Queen continued on through the States, taking in the usual mixture of official engagements, church services, parades, and what have you. Next was

Broken Hill, then Queensland and then the Barrier Reef. A flight southwest took her to Adelaide. **But there the Royal Party got quite a shock.**

DISAPPOINTMENT IN PERTH

When the Queen arrived in Adelaide, she received some surprising mail. It was from parents and their various representative bodies in WA **requesting the Queen not to visit that State.** The reason was that they thought that **polio** in the State had reached alarming proportions, and they worried that **the Queen might become infected**. They were also concerned that the gatherings of children together would spread the disease.

Polio was a very frightening disease, and every parent in 1954 was conscious that their children were seriously at a small risk of being affected. The epidemic had come and never completely gone for a few years, and it seemed to have fresh legs in the last two months. With the tour only a week away from Perth, officials started considering the possibility of varying the tour, or maybe canceling it.

Most Western Australians were aghast at the thought of altering anything. They argued that the disease was no more prevalent there than it had been throughout all of Australia, and there was no need for panic measures. Still it was hard to ignore the evidence. For example, on March 23rd, 18 new cases of polio were reported in WA, and that brought the total for the month to 168. This was more than twice the previous month's total of 80.

Our Prime Minister then stepped in. He announced that the tour would be modified. The new plan was that the Queen and Duke and the entire Royal Party would live aboard the

Brittania, instead of in the land-based Government House. Practically all indoor functions would be cancelled. The Royal Party would in future eat only food carried in reserve by the ship, and prepared on the ship, and no local produce. Shaking of hands would be eliminated. Children would not be permitted to make presentations, such as bouquets, to the Queen. Public functions, such as the Royal Ball, would be cancelled.

So, at the beginning of April, a British ship sailed into one of our harbours, and dropped anchor. Various forays inland were made by occasional day-parties, but they were always careful to be back before dark. They ate only food brought from England with them, and prepared by their own cooks. Contact with the friendly staring natives was limited to essentials, though an English Guard was always at the ready to maintain law and order. **Who said history does not repeat itself?**

CAN TOPSY COUNT?

Some old-timers like myself will remember the various travelling shows that featured magicians of all sorts. One couple I can remember particularly was the Pilkingtons, who were part of the entertainment scene for decades. The male Pilkington was the magician type, and his wife would put on blindfolds, or get into closets where she could not see, or go outside the theatre, and somehow project some information about random patrons to the male. He in turn would reveal the patron's little life secrets, and we would all go away amazed and happy. It was a great act.

Given how popular such acts were, it is not too surprising to find the occasion **animal** got in on them.

Letters, J Sloan. With reference to S Yudovitch's doubts about animal intelligence, I saw the pony Topsy at Surfers Paradise, and was advised to watch the keeper for a sign that would make Topsy stop stamping her feet.

I watched the keeper intently and he did not drop an eyelid. This gave me and 10 others the impression that Topsy can count.

Letters, M A W. I attended a show given by the pony, Topsy, and her owner at Surfers' Paradise and I lost confidence in Topsy's educational attainments when her owner attributed to her a degree of knowledge and interest which was obviously absurd.

Some of us came away convinced that Topsy had been taught two things: when to lift her foot and when to stop lifting it, and when to shake her head from side to side and when to move it up and down. With those two points mastered, the rest was easy.

Letters, R Garling, Collaroy. The suggestion made by S. Yudovitch does not measure up with the investigations of a number of members, including myself, of the *International Brotherhood of Magicians*. In Queensland last year I had a long discussion with Mr Arthur Prince, of Southport, who has seen the pony, Topsy, perform on a number of occasions. Mr Prince is an exceptionally well-informed magician, and he and other magicians have found that it is not necessary for Topsy's owner to be in the pony's line of vision to give correct answers to questions. Actually, the secret is far more subtle and the performance really remarkable.

Letters, Jean Garling. I have been interested in letters about the performance of the pony, Topsy. My relative, Rus Garling, commends it from the aspect of professional magicians, and M A W slights it.

In my research into the history of dance, I followed up horse ballet work, which is based on the same technical training as in tricks. This depends on the reaction of a horse to signs, and the animal's ability to respond depends on its reflexes, which vary considerably. Not many horses have quick enough reflexes to enter the show business, which even then is achieved only after patient and prolonged training.

I watched Topsy, and while it was impossible for the eye to take in the owner's method of giving signs, there was, as Mr Garling suggests, a definite and subtle link between the two.

When I saw Topsy she was nervous, and kept looking at her foal standing nearby. This at times caused her to miss a correct answer. But there was remarkable evidence of high reflex development in her.

Comment. Can Topsy count? We still don't know.

NEWS AND VIEWS

Letters, Bucephalus. The official decision to replace Sydney's double-decker buses with the single-decker type has been received with remarkable silence.

The reason for the change which has been offered by the Department is that passengers are averse to climbing the stairs to the upper deck – surely as unconvincing an explanation as has ever been put forward. Mounting a short flight of stairs is a small price to pay for the comfort of a part of the bus in which standing passengers are not permitted, and where, moreover, smokers may most conveniently be segregated from non-smokers. The Department's alternative plan is to reduce considerably the seating facilities and double the number of strap-hangers, so that those who are seated may have their good fortune diminished by being trampled upon.

In London, where the peak period in the evening lasts for almost two hours, it has not been found necessary to decimate reasonable seating accommodation as an unwarranted luxury.

Since no intelligible reason can be found for the general introduction of single-decker buses, it would appear that in this respect the citizens of Sydney are once more being offered a stone in the place of bread.

NEWS AND VIEWS

One thousand school children in Casino have gone on strike, refusing to drink the free milk provided for the schools. They say that the region is great for dairying, but they are getting low-grade watered milk. They will not drink it until it improves. In true union style, there were no dissenters at all.

APRIL NEWS ITEMS

April 6th. NSW will this week pass laws that will allow **petrol stations to trade at any hour of the day or night, seven days a week**. The legislation will definitely be passed by Thursday, and receive the Governor's signature on Friday, so said the Premier, Mr Cahill.

April 5th. Following **successful testing of H-bombs** in the Pacific, America has now gone into **full scale production of them**. People world-wide will now sleep secure in the knowledge that the world is a safer place….

April 8th. The science expert of the New York Times said today that the hydrogen-bomb testing proved it **was now possible to develop a cobalt bomb**. This means that Albert Einstein's prediction that a bomb could be developed that would destroy all human life was now within reach….

"On being vaporised in the explosion, the cobalt casing would be transformed into a **deadly radio-active cloud 320 times more powerful than radium**. This cloud would travel with the prevailing winds thousands of miles, **destroying all life in its path**." By using several cobalt bombs, all human life could be destroyed.

Oh goody. There will be **a Federal election** next month.

April 8th. The NSW Premier announced that, after talks with Trade Unions, **the relaxing of trading hours for petrol stations would be delayed** until the Parliamentary sitting in August. He also said that probably the time of trading would be increased by a few hours daily, and **not become 24-hours a day**.

Continuing **the H-bomb scare** campaign, Australian Professor Marcus Oliphant said that "there is no defence against atomic weapons unless humanity is prepared to live, work, and grow food deep **beneath the surface of the earth**."

April 9th. The **pearling season** started in Darwin today.

By the end of April, **Senator Joe McCarthy was in trouble**. His Committee for UnAmerican Activities had been trying to **persecute anyone who might or might not have Communist affiliations**.   But he had gone miles too far, even in America....

The President, the Secretary of State, and other high officials **recently told him to pull his head in**, in no uncertain terms. He had reacted defiantly and it appeared that a head-on battle was looming. At the end of the month, the US Army was in direct conflict with him, and his position had deteriorated. **Was his infamous reign of terror coming to an end?**

At the Sydney Royal Easter Show, there were **only two entrants in the toffee-making section**. Several writers were sad that the **art of making toffee** was being lost.

A writer observed that the average **cormorant ate over 100 small fish a day**. He claimed that it was silly to restrict anglers to a small number of fish per day. Instead, he said, **kill the birds**.

H-BOMBS AND THEIR FALL-OUT

During April, the controversy over the US exploding H-bombs in the Pacific kept growing. The familiar US defence of the practice was that the "free world" was under threat from the Communists. It was clearly only by having bombs of huge magnitude that the Reds would be deterred from attacking, and that bigger and better **tested** bombs were necessary to keep up with the Russians. The word **"deterrence"** was used over and over.

There were dozens and dozens of arguments for and against this position, but that was where America had settled, and there was really no argument that would change its mind. So, for example, while it was obvious that the recent bombs tests had condemned over 100 Japanese sailors to slow death by radium-like contamination, and had permanently destroyed the habitats of thousands of Pacific Islanders, America stuck to its policy of obvious deterrence. At the end of April, it made it clear that the series of tests would go ahead as planned over the next few months.

The normally apathetic people of Australia usually took little notice of news about atom bombs. They had heard so many scare stories since **WWII** that it was just ho-hum to them. Newspaper articles on bombs and mushroom clouds by now only got to about 24 column-inches in the papers, and then scarcely made Page 3. But this time, many people got quite stirred up. I have included a Letter from a Mr Baker that moved the discussion down an unusual path.

Letters, George Baker. Letters from two professors recently said that the hydrogen bomb was a bad thing, and that it should be banned.

If the learned gentlemen have a workable scheme for banning the bomb - a scheme safe for us and acceptable to the Communists - the world will listen to them with some attention. But if they have no scheme, why did they put pens to paper? They would have been wiser to refrain lest what they wrote should tempt the Communists with an impression of Western disunity and uncertainty of purpose.

He went on to say that if the world comes to an impasse over how to remove the menace of the bombs, then we should "stick to our bombs", and be prepared for an all-out nuclear war.

If we made any further concession, we should be delivering ourselves bound into their hands. **To most of us this fate seems more terrible than the risk of death by fission, by incineration, or by radioactive poisoning.**

This is a strong statement. He suggests that **we would be better off dead than being subservient to the Communist State**. Quite a few writers had something to say on this.

Letters, Gray and Margaret Senior. Mr Baker's final statement, evidently considered to be a responsible and rational claim, surely reached an incredible zenith in sophistry. If for most of us death is our choice, faced with the alternative of life under a different social system, human intelligence has indeed abandoned itself to cowardice, fear, and self-annihilation.

If Mr Baker's assessment of "most of us" is correct may two of the minority publicly disclaim this ambition and, of his alternatives, choose life, hope and endeavour under any political system whatsoever.

Letters, Pat Peck. Mr Baker, may know what "most of us" are thinking: I do not; but I think that the instinct of self-preservation is stronger than is the fear of subjugation by any ideology. I find it hard to endure any of the political or social arrangements of our day, but I do not take my life because of that, nor do I advocate the extinction of the human race.

Our task, at the very least, is to keep the armed truce of our time, and to persevere in seeking peace. If we fail to find a way for human beings to live together in a peace based on truth, justice, and charity, then perhaps our children may do so.

Letters, H Raymond. Your correspondences of April 13 lack imagination; Mr Baker receives my support. To be dead does not really matter, but to be alive in helpless misery does.

Letters, I Gronowski. I agree with the view expressed by Gray and Margaret Senior that for most Australians life seems worth living even if we were under Communist domination.

Where I disagree with these correspondents is in the part of the letter in which they try to show Communist domination as simply a different political and social system. **Communism is something more than that**; it is a doctrine which dehumanises man as a human being and tries to kill his soul by denying its existence in the first place and poisoning it in the next. This is a very real danger for the humanity as a whole, not smaller than the H-bomb itself. Some people, who realise it, would rather lose their life than become, and let their children become, living automates and lose everything which is dear and sacred to them.

Comment. Most writers agreed that life under subjegation was preferable to no life at all. But there were enough people who disagreed with that to make me realise, once again, that the **popular voice** is not always the **universal voice**.

Second comment. Returning to the general question of deterrence, the American policy of "massive deterrence" was only one on many such policies. **For example**, another would have been for America to ignore the various bombs, and not make any at all. The logic here was that if the Russians **did** go ahead and drop bombs anywhere in the world, the radiation clouds would float over them inside a week, and they knew they would be just as dead as their targets would be. This was another form of deterrence. Though this particular form had no realistic chance of implementation, because there is no money in **not** making bombs. Capitalism, we are told, needs innovation to survive.

There were many critics of **massive deterrence** policy, and most of these stayed critical for decades as the Cold War got hotter and then colder. Still, when we look back from 2016 say, it must be admitted that **something** has worked. That is, there has been no atomic catastrophe in the entire world in that period. Whether it was because of this American policy, or one of several other ploys, that staved off the terrible day, is open to argument. But somehow the world, despite all its inanities, has muddled through what was really a very dangerous period – **so far.**

OUR VERY OWN SPY

This was a period when it was very fashionable for various nations to have spy dramas. The Americans and Russians were already old hands at this, and recently the Canadians had been allowed their own. To the British, Kilby and Burgess and McClean were household names.

Australia as a nation thought we were too far out of the Big League to have our own spies. In any case, so we thought, what was there in Oz that someone would want to spy on? We had just established the cloak and dagger team at ASIO to protect the nation, and surely that would be enough. Sadly, it seemed, we were destined only to read about the thrills of espionage in spy novels and the overseas news.

Then, out of the blue, our Prime Minister Menzies stepped in. He came out with a solemn announcement that a diplomat, called Vladimir Petrov, had defected from the Russian Embassy, and was seeking asylum in Oz. As part of the deal he would bring papers that would expose the details of his activities, and the names of other spies. We also found out later that Petrov would be paid for his information, and given a new identity when he had done his bit.

Oh joy. What bliss. We had our own spy. Our reaction was typically Australian. There was no worry at all about what damage the rascals were perpetrating, no thoughts about what vital secrets could be divulged. It was rather exciting and maybe hilarious that such a promising episode was happening here. Right here. Not in Whitehall, nor the Kremlin, nor in Washington nor the Pentagon, where spies preferred to work. Rather, in the dark and seamy corridors of Canberra, in the burgled offices in Sydney's Eastern Suburbs, in the local RSL club where you would expect spies in trench-coats to rendezvous and flit in and out.

So we waited for details. Menzies released information that told us that Petrov had gone into hiding in Government custody, that names of spies were not yet available, and that he had sent messages to the Russian Ambassador noting his disquiet. He did not know the whereabouts of Mrs Petrov.

Over the next few days, the normal spy things happened. Diplomats were withdrawn from Oz and Russia and sent home. The Russians were accused of all sorts of silly things, as were the Australians in Russia. Then Menzies easily won the support of Parliament for a Royal Commission into the whole affair. Even Doc Evatt, of the Labor Party, agreed .

But the drama was yet to come. On the 20th of April, Mrs Petrov was seen being pushed into a car in Canberra. She turned up with two Russian heavies at Sydney airport, and was dragged crying and protesting onto a commercial plane. She lost both shoes in the process, and was not allowed to regather them. It looked as if she was being kidnapped. On the flight to Darwin, a stewardess spoke to her in the toilet, and she indicated she was not leaving Australia of her own free will, and that she wanted to stay here.

At Darwin, with the nation's Government now alert to the situation, the hostess reported her conversation, and after playing some ducks and drakes, the Northern Territory Police moved in and brought Mrs Petrov into their custody. The two armed heavies continued on their flight to Moscow. Mrs Petrov was re-united with her husband.

All of this was played out publicly. Wonderful photos of the innocent, kidnapped Mrs Petrov being dragged through a mob to the aircraft in Sydney abounded. Similarly, there were many photos in Darwin of the Police and the tough-looking Russians, almost fighting over Mrs Petrov. Thick-necked Russians in heavy suits seemed to spring out of thin air, and the fine-looking Australian constables were clearly displayed in full uniform.

Letters, I McDougall, Secretary, Sane Democracy League of Australia. Dr Evatt's suggestion that Mrs Petrov was needlessly abandoned to the tender mercies of her Russian escorts at Mascot is naïve. It is obvious that Australian Security officers had no right whatever to interfere with Mrs. Petrov's journey "home" until her attitude suggested she was removed against her will.

On the other hand, the selection of Darwin as the venue for a showdown was a highly commendable piece of strategy. Had Sydney been selected, the Russian authorities could have returned Mrs Petrov to the Embassy at Canberra.

Surely most Australians, unlike Dr Evatt, are proud of the manner in which their government spiked the Russian guns.

Letters, Rosina Shaw. Will Dr Evatt, in good taste, refrain from turning this unprecedented and unhappy incident of Mrs Petrov's staying in Australia into a political platform.

This incident has, to my mind, been soul shocking to the women of the free world, and thought provoking to all. For anyone to seize it in order to build a case against a political opponent is to my mind lamentable.

Letters, Old Australian. In my opinion, the situation was handled efficiently. Mrs. Petrov obviously could not make up her mind at Mascot. Her decision was of vital importance, and there could be no reversal once it was made. No wonder she hesitated. It would have been criminal for anyone in authority here to interfere. The decision was hers and hers alone.

Let us have done with carping and criticism, and congratulate ourselves on the possession of a good vigilant Security and a fine statesman in the person of our Prime Minister.

Letters, Pax. May the Darwin liberation be a symbol of a much greater liberation. It came like a practical revelation of the Easter message: that evil shall not be met with evil, but with love.

Letters, F J Browne. If, as seems more than likely, Mrs Petrov was drugged before leaving Canberra, it shows superlative wisdom on the part of the Federal authorities that they delayed official interrogation until her arrival at Darwin when her mind would be less confused. Questioning at Mascot might have resulted in a completely wrong interpretation of her wishes.

Letters, G L Burgoyne. Physical intervention at Mascot might have precipitated a riot, with possible bloodshed and serious international consequences.

Nothing was lost by delaying action until the quiet atmosphere of Darwin was reached.

When the dust settled, the Petrovs were in hiding in Australia somewhere, in the custody of the Government, and awaiting a Royal Commission. Their longer-term fate was a complete unknown, except it was certain they would have to appear at the Commission. The glamour of our spy drama had gone, but there was still the political aftermath to come. In the next few months, as we will see, there was a ton of drama ahead with lots of fallout that **put paid to the political ambitions of one of our leading politicians.**

THE FEDERAL ELECTIONS

In a few weeks, the nation was going to the polls. It looked like it would be a drab affair. The Liberal Party, supported by the Country Party, was now in power, and was ready to argue that **its economic management had been good enough** to gain an extension of office. The Labor Party had a collection of promises that were aimed deliberately at gaining the working man's vote, and criticised the many obvious failures of the economic management that the Liberals were ostensibly so proud of. In short, neither Party had a creative vision for Australia, and it was obvious that whoever won, we would just keep muddling through, happily enough, if the world left us alone.

In the absence of any clear policies to campaign on, **the Leaders** of the Parties became conspicuous. Bob Menzies, for the Liberals, was respected by all for his eloquence and obvious intelligence, but huge numbers had hated him since the beginning of WWII, for some policies he had implemented at the start of the War. "Pig-iron Bob" was the cry wherever he went.

The Labor Party had three leaders who revolted equally huge numbers of voters on the other side. Evatt, Calwell and Ward between them could muster millions of voters who thought they were just plain ratbags. These men hoped they could win office by simply hurling mud at their opponents, and had no idea of creating policies that would stand the least scrutiny.

So, at the beginning of May, the pollies were just about ready to start their campaigns. Probably, a betting-man would have thought that the Parties were both about "even money" in this two-horse race. Though, he would have felt a bit uneasy, because there was one possibly disturbing event due to start before the elections. That was the Petrov Royal Commission, and what **it** might come up with was **anyone's guess.**

PIES AND TOFFEES

Here is a reminder of good things gone forever, perhaps.

Letters, M N Haberfield. I am reminded by your subleader on "The Art of Toffee-making" that some 40 years ago a small cottage converted into a shop sold the most delectable toffee, which people came from far and near to buy. The little house is still in Darlington Road, near Cleveland Street.

The shopkeepers at that time were a Mr and Mrs Toogood. He was large, genial, bearded, twinkly-eyed and very kind to children. His wife was small and thin and wore her hair in a bun on the nape of her neck. The toffee for which the little shop was renowned, was made by the lady, on the premises.

Local youngsters always carefully watched until Mr Toogood was behind the counter, because he gave larger pennyworth than did his spouse. This glorious toffee was the colour of barley sugar, and crackled when bitten, or, if sucked slowly, extended itself into any lengths which children desired. Because of this flexibility it was affectionately known among the younger buyers as "Toogood's Muck."

The recipe, no doubt, died with its maker.

Letters, Simon A. Your lament for toffee reminds me of another vanishing art, that of the piemaker.

Where are the delicious mutton and pork pies of 30 years and more ago? I am told that the pastry cooks will not now make mutton pies because of the small extra trouble involved in ridding the filling of fat: yet there is nothing like a mutton pie for flavour. Pork pies seem to have vanished for no reason. At least I have been unable to find them anywhere in Sydney. The unimaginative beef pie, often poorly made with lumpy gristle meat instead of a pleasant mince, seems the only available meat pie.

Letters, Nonagenarian. Simon A's letter about the lost art of pie-making took my memory back to the 1870s and the mutton pies made by Mr Holmes of King St. (His name is still on the shop he occupied.)

I was a pupil at Fort Street School in those days and with many other boys bought pies from Mr Holmes. He was a kindly old man and delighted in seeing the boys helping themselves from a big pile of pies at the end of the counter. "How many did you eat?" he would ask the boys and a few with big appetites but little cash would say "two" after sinking four. Mr Holmes would know but, with a kindly twinkle in his eyes, would not question them further.

His pies were succulent and brown. I have never seen their like since, and feel sure I never will.

NEWS AND VIEWS

Letters, Edward Hirst. At about 8 o'clock this morning at a holiday resort near Sydney I saw a fully grown male native bear on the ground about two yards from the verandah. He climbed up a rough iron-bark tree, then jumped five feet across to a grey gum and settled down in a fork about 30 feet up.

Shortly afterwards a three-quarter grown bear, a male, appeared and followed the old gentleman up the tree.

A fight ensued – a boxing bout – and the young bear was finally driven off. During the fight, the old bear made deep grunting noises, and whenever he was hit the younger bear cried like a child.

During the fight, four currawongs came along and made assaults upon the two bears. It almost appeared as if they were going for the bears' eyes, or at least trying to pull their characteristic ears.

Have any of your readers experienced a similar fight in daylight?   And what can the reason be for the currawongs being so interested?

News report, May 31st. The Queen caught three salmon when she went fishing on the River Dee during a 10-day holiday at Balmoral Castle.

Hollywood comedian, **Charlie Chaplin**, was granted a **Russian** Peace Prize. He is already under severe criticism in America for **his pro-Communist leanings**, and this will (and did) damage his reputation further.

The Chairman of the Joint Coal Board stated that **200 miners in northern NSW fields would lose their jobs**, because of **over-production**. For most of the last 15 years, the shortage of coal has been a constant torment for all of Australia, and **miners' strikes had become something you could rely on. What will the newspapers do if they can't bash the miners for striking?**

MAY NEWS ITEMS

Walt Disney, in America, announced that he is building a combination of world fair, playground, community centre, museum of living facts, and a showplace of beauty and magic. **He will call it "Disneyland".**

Jimmy Carruthers retained his world bantamweight boxing title in a fight against Thai boxer Songkitrat.

The NSW Department of Government has said that, in future, **it will enforce its ban** on smoking in non-smoking sections of trams and busses. "Passengers suffering from lung complaints have become ill from the effects of tobacco smoke." **There was no hint of recognition of the link with cancer.**

Jimmy Carruthers on May 17th announced that he **will retire from boxing.** He was a rare boxer because he retired undefeated, and apparently **not yet damaged by his fights**. He went on to buy the Bells Hotel at Rushcutters Bay in Sydney.

The NSW Railways announced that it would **repaint all of its railway stations, and that brighter colours** would be used. Such colours as cream, white, green, orange and yellow would be used. This would get away from the drab stone colour that the stations had used previously.

Chiang Kai Shek, re-elected as President of **off-shore Formosa**, pledged that **he would suppress China's Communist revolt,** and would rejuvenate the nation.

He was being **given massive support by the USA**, and **his empty threats to China** were taken seriously and hopefully for a decade by the US.

May 24th. Police were warning of the dangers of **cracker night**. This wonderful night for the kids was always marred by injuries. **In a few years, it was curtailed by safety regulations**, and the fun went out of it.

The six o'clock swill in pubs is still alive and well. Now, a Staff Correspondent with the *SMH* reported that in our cities there is **a one o'clock swill** as well....

This swill occurs **in milk bars** as thousands of young girls are released from offices for their lunch. **He talks of standing four deep at counters,** waiting to get served. Apparently, the young ones do not retire when served, but stand at the bar drinking till they have finished....

He adds that they do this in solemn mood, and rarely speak even to their companions. When they leave, they always **turn their straw over the edge of the glass**, as if to prevent its re-use. He opines that **the frothiness of the shake** has much **deteriorated over the years** because of the great haste in which it was prepared.

The BBC reported that it had put to air a programme from **Lebanon that recorded a Bedouin marriage ceremony**. It mentioned that the bride had never seen her husband before, and that she was led in on a horse. But the part that got it all excited was the price it had to pay for **the rights to the broadcast: five sheep**.

GET RID OF THE MEANS TEST

At the end of the month, the nation was to go to the polls to elect a new government for Australia. This was to be a simple two-horse race. On the one hand, the Labor Party, with its trade union affiliations, and its working class support, was still pushing its war-time ideals of socialisation. Unfortunately for them, this brought them very close to the current bogey-men, the Reds, who were looking to impose a very severe form of socialism, called Communism. Bob Menzies, the Liberal leader, forever drumming up fears of Communism, was using it to smear the largely-innocent Labor stalwarts.

On the other hand, the Liberals, in bed with the rural-based Country Party, were the incumbents, and were blithely espousing free enterprise, and liberal capitalism, and at the same time, dispensing enough money to social services to provide a safety net for the battlers in society. For example, over the last decade or so, they had made decent provisions for old age pensions, and for child endowment.

With the election coming up, it was clear that there was nothing really wrong with Oz society or the economy, so it was hard for the challengers, the Labor Party, to campaign on the dissatisfaction in society. Then again, it was hard to campaign on grandiose plans for the future development of the nation. This was because the Labor Party had none of these. So Doctor Evatt, the Leader, **proposed that the means test on pensions should be abolished, in its entirety.**

I need to explain a little about the means test. The whole idea of a pension was to provide a reasonable income to workers after they reached their age of retirement from paid employment. So the ordinary Joe Blow would turn 65, and get a weekly payment, called a pension, for the rest of his life. It would probably be only a third of what he was getting before he retired, but it kept body and soul together.

Life, however, is never that simple. The objection was raised that richer men would benefit from this scheme if payments were made to everyone. So, the means test was introduced. Simply put, this meant that anyone with assets over a certain limit would not get a pension. That, so the reasoning went, was because they did not need the money. After all, this argument went, the money was coming from taxpayers, and why should they be forced to pay pensions to the wealthy?

There were dozens of arguments against imposing the test. For example, suppose a man worked and saved hard all of his life, and thus accumulated assets. When he retired, he would not get the pension because of these assets. He had done the right thing all his life, and paid a mountain of taxes. Yet, at the end he would not get a pension, but the idle wastrel would. Where, it was argued, was the justice in this?

Another common complaint was that the family home was included in the definition of assets. What about the man who had paid off his house, but then had no other assets. He would get no pension, and would have to survive probably by selling his house. Where was the justice now?

If these arguments got complex, now Dr Evatt's proposal stirred them up even more. This small sample shown below just scratched the surface among Letter writers.

Letters, John Collins. In the discussion on the means test, nobody has even mentioned the old fellow-citizens debarred by law from any old age pension, means test or no means test, even if they are completely destitute, simply because they have **not yet lived 20 years in their adopted country**.

Nobody can expect that every naturalised citizen should become eligible for the pension on the day he takes oath of allegiance, but 10 years' residence had to be enough to qualify him and any person over 70 should be treated alike in this regard.

Letters, Rev Robin Blair. The fundamental reason for the granting of pensions should be remembered by us all in this scramble to possess more money. It was **to help the poorest citizens in our community** who, whether through misfortune, age, or illness, urgently needed our Christian help. "In as much as ye do it unto these, the poorest of My brethren, ye do it unto Me." This need has never been more necessitous than to-day, and the fact remains that our first and vital consideration should not be to provide more for those who have, but to see that all those who have not, are taken care of.

Letters, D Chater. I would like to remind Mr Geoffrey Smith that there are thousands of retired citizens on less than the amount that gentleman claims is necessary for decent living, and who, if they do have to live quietly and practice many self-denials, **do not expect to be supported at the country's expense**.

Letters, J Curle. Australians would destroy their own democracy. They demand too much from the State, and they always elect men of poor moral fibre who give it to them as a bribe.

Letters, Iris Hale. Of all the groups of pensioners surely the worst cases of hardship occur among widows with young children. For a civilian widow with one child the amount is £3/15/ per week. With rents at an all-time high and food and clothing also at high rates, surely this is a totally inadequate amount.

The mother invariably starves herself in an effort to provide for her young. It will be said she is "permitted" to earn an extra £2, but very often cannot leave her young children alone to go to work.

There is no place she can go to obtain relief upon the death of the breadwinner such as is available to the war widow, and in many cases **the pension takes five or six months to come through**.

During this period she must exist and provide for her children as best she might. The Social Service, both State and Commonwealth, can do nothing for her. She fills in questionnaires by the dozen. The Child Welfare cannot help. "She has applied for a pension." How she is to exist until it materialises no one knows or cares.

Surely there should be a place where the widow upon loss of the breadwinner should be able to apply for immediate help.

Letters, Michael Sawtell, Aborigines' Welfare Board of NSW. This election will be fought mainly around the question of pensions.

Therefore, I would like publicly to ask what is the attitude of Mr Menzies and Dr Evatt towards the granting of pensions to the **aged, full-blood, detribalised and non-exempted aborigines** now living on Government stations and reserves but who are at present debarred from the Federal pensions?

Letters, E Nancy. As the wife of a retired superannuated clergymen, whose income was "fixed" 16 years ago, I should be one of the first to go to the poll on Saturday, determined to vote for the party that has promised to abolish the means test at once.

If I thought of myself and not of my country, I would do this. Being a sane, thinking woman, however, I recall, with thankfulness, the results of the present Menzies Liberal Government's action in the past three years after they took over from the Labor Government in the days when we women had daily "headaches" trying to cope with running the home on shortages, under-the-counter tactics, and all the rest of it. To-day we no longer suffer these indignities; on the contrary, we are almost back to the good old days which most of us thought were surely beyond recall. We women can trust a Government which has brought us through the mire. The Government's word is good enough for me and the Menzies Government will abolish the means test gradually, and in the meantime will grant a substantial easing thereof.

Comment. Menzies reckoned that cutting out the test would be popular with some better-off elements in society, but he reckoned that the economic folly of doing that, for the nation, would be recognised. He also remembered that the initial purpose of the pension provision was **to establish a safe base for the impoverished.** If anomalies and contradictions abounded, he still argued that it was better to keep the pension as it was, rather than to try to fix it, and then maybe destroy the safe haven effect than it was providing for the truly needy. Curiously enough, this was a very socialistic approach, though, he would have hastened to add, not at all Communistic.

I think it would be true to say that anyone reading this book would know that the means test on the old-age pension has not been abolished. In fact, due to the massive increase in the numbers of persons on superannuation, it has become a never-ending source of sport played between the government and its citizens, as the latter try to keep up with, and out-fox, the various moves by the former.

THE HEAVY ROAD TOLL

Towards the end of May, it was announced that a special conference would be held to discuss the rising number of road deaths in NSW. This was becoming an increasing problem in all States, and the authorities all over the nation were trying to reduce the number.

In NSW, the Police and Road Transport Department and other experts would be in attendance, but it seemed that they had all met before and not come up with solutions. There was, however, a multitude of suggested solutions from ordinary civilians available, and they rushed into print to suggest what should be done.

Letters, D McDonald. Every careful motorist knows that the rapid increase in the number of traffic accidents is due mainly to the high percentage of incompetent, reckless, and drunken drivers on Australian roads. He also knows that under present conditions, State traffic authorities have little, if any, chance of curbing the activities of these dangerous drivers.

In each State the Road Safety Council or Traffic Department should set up a central Bureau whose specific function is to deal with unsafe driving. If a motorist notices a motor vehicle being driven in a dangerous manner, he should have the opportunity of reporting his observations (description of car and driver, registration number, location, time, date, etc.) to the Bureau. It is certain that an instance of dangerous driving would be noticed by other motorists who also should inform the Bureau. It should not be long, therefore, before the Bureau had sufficient reports enabling it to have reliable records of:

1. Careful drivers whose reports, upon investigation, are found to be reliable and trustworthy.

2. Bad drivers whose dangerous practices are constantly being reported and against whom measures can be taken.

3. Ordinary motorists who (like myself) unintentionally make mistakes and who are unaware unless their attention is drawn to them.

The method as set out above has been in operation in certain States of the USA for several years and, I understand, has proved an outstanding success.

Letters, 30 Years' Motoring. Why is it that when the road toll is discussed there is always a noticeable reluctance to acknowledge the major cause of accidents. That is, speed.

Time and again competent authorities have pointed out that speed is the culprit, yet no sooner is this mentioned than all kinds of people, including many motorists, attempt hard to discount it. Carelessness, incompetence, and drunkenness are of course underlying causes of accidents, but the direct cause is nearly always a rate of speed too high in given circumstances.

To-day, the majority of motorists are constantly exceeding the 30 mph limit and the careless minority are breaking it flagrantly. If we are serious about cutting down the accident rate, then we must cut down the speed rate. If the present speed laws were enforced, that alone would bring about a great improvement.

Unhappily, this vital truth is obscured by those who talk about the improved control, stability and braking power of the modern car and who make these factors an excuse for advocating raised speed limits. This is tragic reasoning. Humans are humans and speed is speed. And speed is what causes accidents and makes their consequences so deadly.

Letters, Veteran. A person is entitled to be in a hurry sometimes and when he is frustrated by timid or selfish drivers it is human nature that he takes a chance and breaks regulation.

I am not a slow driver. I have driven at over 80 mph, and in trials, but I have had 36 years' driving with a clean sheet, and I put this down to a rigid regard for the regulations, especially at halt signs, intersections, pedestrian crossings; overtaking near corners or the crest of a hill; a respect for the other road users; and, last but not least, plain commonsense.

Letters, M Allen, Pedestrians' Road Safety League, Sydney. Despite the immense reduction in deaths on our NSW roads that followed the introduction of the 30 mph speed limit, the Police Department and the Department of Motor Transport have fought against the introduction of further limitation.

The existing 50 mph prima facie limit is a pure delusion, because the police are powerless to prevent motorists from speeding up to 100 mph outside street-lit areas.

As soon as speed limits are mentioned at safety conferences, motor trade interests, which usually have an unduly big representation, get up in arms against them, because vehicles are sold largely on sales talk about high speeds. The authorities must sooner or later wake up to the need for speed control and cease to sneer at every attempt made to discuss freely and scientifically the element of speed in road fatalities.

Letters, RR. All the machinery of driving is kept in reasonably good repair except the drivers.

The minimum age for holding licenses should be made 20 for males and 25 for females, and there should be a compulsory driving test for all licensed drivers every five years.

The maximum age for holding a license should be 65 unless a difficulty test of competency is passed, and passed every succeeding year.

Letters, License No. 2692. A stiff penalty, including gaol, should be imposed on any car thief, whether or not he causes injury or loss of life.

The inebriated driver should be dealt with in the severest possible manner. The present method of testing applicants for driving licenses should be considerably tightened.

Pedestrians should have it impressed upon them that they must not consider to have prior rights when traffic is congested, and should not rely on the ability of the motorist to avoid them because they choose to be dilatory in their movements.

Letters, G S Stanley. I was appalled at some of the suggestions made at the conference convened by the Commissioner of Police.

There has been a marked tendency lately for people in high places to clamour for regression and not progression. It is **simple to impose penalties** on people rather than seek a constructive and permanent solution to a difficult problem, which would preserve and not destroy whatever civil rights still exist.

Comment. On a population basis, road death rates are a lot lower in 2016 than they were sixty years earlier. This is because of seat belts, the drink-driving limits, safer cars, and better roads, and better driver education. It drives home the point that social change can be brought about by the persistent determination of government and society, and the appropriate use of technology. Yet, the road toll figures are still too high, and the number of young males killed each year still makes experts everywhere wonder how these young men, and their families and victims, can be saved from themselves.

ELECTION RESULTS

The Liberals won the election by about eight seats, about 63 to 55. Doc Evatt's many promises did not work for him, as the urbane Bob Menzies did not try to match him in the give-away stakes. Once again the Oz electorate was not convinced by promises of grand futures, and of free benefits, and voted for the solid dependable government of the Liberals.

In fact, it voted that way for more than the next decade and a half, and it was not until the excitement of a new Labor Leader, Gough Whitlam, that Labor was voted back into power after 16 years in Opposition..

MORE ON TOFFEE

Letters, W Toogood, Croydon Park. Being a nephew and the only surviving relative of the Toogoods of Darlinghurst, I was very pleased to read your comments on their celebrated coffee. I can well remember them making their toffee, also helping at times. The boys at Darlington school greatly enjoyed it, buying it by the halfpenny worth.

They also had a large cat who was a sort of guardian of the shop, and whose diet was chiefly biscuits.

Letters, M G, Forbes. All the toffee shops of nostalgic memories were not in Sydney.

I recall, and no doubt others with me, just such a shop in George Street, Bathurst – Croft's Lolly Shop. On the days when the toffee was made, huge slabs of amber streaked with beige whirls, plain dark and light, and also bright pink coconut ice, appeared in the glass case. It was broken up by the jolly Mr Croft, or his wife, into "penn'orths" for the hordes of schoolchildren who were daily patrons.

Letters, W Johnson. Letters about toffee shops have reminded me of Emmets toffee shop in Balmain, close to the Darling Road school. It sold "stickjaw" and prizes were given to children for making all kinds of objects from the stickjaw, those being exhibited to attract more custom.

Letters, E P Davidson, Croydon. Hundreds, possibly thousands, will remember Bailey's toffee shop opposite Ashfield school.

The great speciality there was the "chew-de-cud" (honeycomb), raspberry, lemon and honey toffee. Wrapped in newspaper, we stuffed it into our sailor coats, where the elastic waistband kept it secure and while our lessons were in progress we surreptitiously ate it.

Often we were brought out in front of the class and given two, four or even a "sixer" with the cane for eating in school.

NEWS ITEMS AND TRIVIA

Letters, G Sturrock. In a recent issue of the "Herald" appeared a picture of two children wearing war medals and ribbons.

It is not widely enough known that the wearing of British service medals or ribbons by persons other than those to whom they were awarded is illegal. The Returned Soldiers' League does not possess the right, as some members think it does, to grant permission to anybody to wear service medals or ribbons on Anzac Day or at an Anzac function.

There exists no right whatever for children, wives, widows or any other person to wear unearned service medals or ribbons without the personal sanction of the Sovereign, which is granted so rarely that there are no known instances in Australia at present.

Letters, War Widow.   This week I visited the Shrine in Hyde Park. Of five men there, four wore hats inside the Shrine, the fifth had no hat with him so he gets the benefit of the doubt.

Surely it is little to ask that in this place men carry out the gesture of reverence and respect for those who died to give us the good life we enjoy in this privileged country.

JUNE NEWS ITEMS

Fruit barrows were a common feature of our cities. Sydney had almost 100 of them. They were in the news because one barrowman had been found to possess two barrows, and that was a breach of Council Rules.

A reminder too that they were brought to and from the city **daily by draught horses** that were tethered in the city for the day. You should also remember that **concrete horse troughs** were in place all along access roads to the city to give these, and other horses, a drink.

A final reminder. These horse troughs were spread right across the nation, especially in country areas. **Can anyone tell me where they all went?**

Prime Minister Menzies, summing up the elections said "the results show that this is **a community that prefers steady progress on sound foundations** to taking a chance of getting something for nothing."

News report, June 11th. A preliminary hearing of the Royal Commission into **the Petrov spy case was adjourned** until June 30th.

Australian sprinter, **John Landy**, was **in Europe** following the athletic meets, and **attempting to break the four-minute mile**, as was recently done by Roger Bannister. Landy was getting to within a few seconds of the four-minutes, but never quite cracking it.

Australian scientists, led by Professor Harry Messel, are talking about **creating nuclear reactors within Australia**. The problem is cost, and what would it do anyway? Messel argues that the scientific applications of nuclear power are developing so rapidly that we should build our own reactors so that we can keep up with the rest of the world.

The English Rugby League team is about to play Test Matches in Australia. Many League stalwarts, from both nations, are greatly upset because **the Brits have appointed an Australian coach for their side**. The Brits are saying that they themselves can coach as well as any Australian. And that the Australian coach will sabotage the Brits. Some Australians are saying **it is treason** for an Australian to help the Brits to win.

Construction work has started on three of the **largest sites to be built for the Olympic games** to be held in Melbourne in November and December, 1956.

Australian tennis pro, **Frank Sedgman**, said he hoped to run a series of **professional tennis matches** in Australia. His group of players would be Richard Gonzales, Pancho Segura, Ken McGregor, and himself.

June 21st. **John Landy broke through the four-minute mile barrier, to claim the world record**. His time was three minutes and 58.0 seconds. He broke the previous record, set by Englishman Roger Bannister last month, of three minutes, 59.4 seconds. The run was made at Turku in Finland, on a specially-fast track made of "black cinders"....

Landy's mother revealed that **Landy had taken his butterfly net with him to Europe** in the hope of adding many beautiful specimens to his already-large collection.

DAME ALICE CHISHOLM

When I was a lad of about 12 years of age, I was fortunate enough to live in the small coal-mining town of Abermain in the Cessnock coalfields. With a population of 2,000, every one of them connected to the mines, there was almost nothing for me to do in the winter evenings except wander up to the local School of Arts to listen to the non-drinking men talk about politics and the past. Some of these were Diggers from WWI, and one topic that came up often was the Egyptian campaign, and within that, there was frequent mention of a canteen at Kantara, and the lady who ran it.

This lady died at the very end of May, and I have indulged myself here by producing a Letter that talked about her and her extraordinary work.

Letters, R.   It would be a gross understatement to affirm that Dame Alice Chisholm, who die on May 30, aged 97, will always be held in affectionate memory by the thousands of Australian Light Horsemen who served in the Sinai and Palestine campaigns in the desert of 1916-1918.

Early in the war, when all Australian troops overseas were concentrated in Egypt, Mrs Chisholm established a canteen in Heliopolis, but this was not the canteen for which she was to become famous.

Early in 1916, three women, including Mrs Chisholm, decided to form, at their own expense, a canteen at Kantara, a lonely outpost on the west bank of the canal. Their intrepid venture was not at first encouraged by the authorities. Miss Rout resigned through illness, but the other two carried on.

One remembers their lone tent, outside it a table and some packing cases, just off the road opposite the pontoon bridge over the canal. This was the setting-out point for all troops entering the fighting zone. Here was true Australian bush hospitality in an unbelievably unique setting. **Did the boys appreciate it!**

As the campaign developed over the years 1916-1918, Kantara became the main base with a permanent population in various depots of 60,000. It was not long before such leaders as Generals Chauvel, Ryrie, and McArthur-Onslow pressed for some official assistance to the two lone ladies. The tiny canteen, a mere mustard seed, blossomed by their energy, devotion and ability into a large hostel. Its growth can be measured by the statement in the official War History of the AIF, that on one occasion 60,000 eggs were cooked in the kitchens in one day. This was an addition to the rations of a whole division camped on route near by.

Late in the campaign, Miss McPhillamy, with General Allenby's consent, established canteens in Jerusalem and, after the armistice, at Rafa. Eventually the financial profits from the canteens involved a sum of considerable size, and the two ladies insisted that it went back to the troops as "comforts": for instance, on troopships taking the boys home. However, a sum was left over and it was donated by Dame Alice to help form the Goulburn Returned Soldiers Club. This club was originally conceived in the mind of the same wonderful lady.

Comment. I can add that Dame Alice was born in 1856, and that her husband died of measles in 1904. Her son was killed in Egypt early in the war, hence her presence in that country. Around 1920, she was awarded various Empire honours, most notably the CBE.

GOOD OLD DIRK HARTOG

While I am indulging myself, I might as well include a second Letter about another interesting person, an explorer, who became a matter for discussion, due to correspondence emanating in the *SMH* at this time.

Letters, A H Chisholm. The Dutch people being noted for thoughtful and kindly actions, it is not surprising to read that the Netherlands Government is presenting to the Commonwealth a piece of plate to mark the fact that 50,000 migrants have transferred from Holland to Australia since 1945.

As a sequel, may I suggest Holland could reasonably go one better by presenting the Hartog Plate to Australia? In doing so it would follow the example of France, which returned the Vlamingh Plate to this country a few years ago?

The Hartog Plate is the oldest known relic of the contact of white men with "New Holland." A circular piece of the pewter about 10 inches in diameter, it was inscribed in 1616 by a Dutch mariner, Dirk Hartog, and nailed upon a post to commemorate his visit to an island (which now bears his name) lying near the west coast of what is now Western Australia.

Eighty-one years later, Willem de Vlamingh (the Dutchman who discovered the Swan River) removed the Hartog memorial and left another in its place, and later again (1817) the French voyager de Freycinet took the Vlamingh Plate to Paris. There it became lost to view until rediscovered in 1945, after which it was presented to Australia by the French Government.

The Hartog Plate, meanwhile, had gone to Batavia and then to Amsterdam, where it found a place in the Royal Colonial Museum. I saw the impressive old relic there in 1938 and was glad to learn later that it had been safeguarded during the German occupation.

A "feeler" I threw out regarding the transfer of the plate to Australia was not cordially received by the museum authorities, but at that time (1938) migration matters were being poorly handled, and Holland, quite justifiably, was a trifle annoyed with Australia. Now the situation is different.

Indeed, with so many Dutch migrants in Australia and, one hopes, many more to come, there is abundant reason for urging that the Hartog Plate, most venerable relic of Dutch contact with this country, should be returned to the land of its origin.

An expression of opinion on this matter by Netherlands authorities would be welcome. If that opinion be favourable, it is to be hoped that the Commonwealth Government will not allow itself to be persuaded, as it did in the case of Vlamingh Plate, to transfer the relic from Canberra to Perth.

Mementos of this nature ought not to be in the possession of any one State. Obviously, they have national significance, and therefore should be held in the national capital.

Letters, C Bellaar Spruyt, Press and Cultural Attache to the Royal Netherlands Embassy.

Mr Chisholm has suggested that the Netherlands Government should present to the Australian Government the famed Hartog Plate, now in the Rysmuseum (National Gallery) at Amsterdam.

This plate is one of the most precious relics from the Golden Age of the Netherlands voyages of discovery and is therefore cherished by the Dutch people as a poignant reminder of the links between our two countries.

In 1938 a bronze replica of the Hartog Plate was presented by the Government of the Netherlands East Indies to the Australian authorities and is now in the possession of the Western Australian Historical Society.

Comment. Dirk Hartog was one of the characters I remember from my sixth-class geography. At the time, it was hard to believe that he had really existed, because **everyone knew** that Australia had been discovered by Captain Cook, and not by Hartog. **Now**, in 1954, a *Herald* Letter stated that he had in fact existed and had been leaving his litter on our beaches in Western Australia, probably the first white man to do so. Still, I don't begrudge him, and I really like the thought that back in 1954, and indeed now, there were people and institutions, here and there, who were consciously doing their best to preserve our history and heritage.

THE SENTENCING OF LEONARD LAWSON

Lawson was a photographer who advertised for models on May 6th, and took five of them into the forest at Terry Hills on Sydney's fringe. He was supposedly intending to photograph them, but he instead tied them up, menaced them with a shotgun, and then raped two or more of them. He was found guilty of rape and other charges, and was sentenced to death June 23rd.

His sentence did not arouse much public comment, because his crime was so reprehensible and was so calculated. Still, his sentence was commuted to 14 years in prison, and this was certainly a sign that **the opposition to the death penalty was widespread in the community**.

An aside. After his release, he raped and killed another model, and killed another girl in a separate event. This time, he was sentenced to life imprisonment, and died in prison in 2003.

A second aside. Lawson was the creator of the well-known comic book series *The Lone Avenger* as well as the other not-so-famous characters of *Diana, Queen of the Apes*, and *Peter Fury*.

LIFE SENTENCE FOR BOYS FOR RAPE

In Sydney, on June 17th, a boy of **14 years, and three others aged 17**, were sentenced **to life imprisonment**, for rape. **This sentence was mandatory in NSW**, whereas on the same day in Queensland the judge had been free to sentence three men, aged 20 to 28 years, to 10 years gaol each for the same crime.

Prelude: This discussion below recognises, as do all the writers quoted below, that rape is a heinous crime and is to be punished severely, and the argument is about the severity of the punishment and what can be done to avoid it.

The *SMH* editorialised with the opinion that mandatory penalties in NSW are archaic and barbarous. It said that had the boys been over 18, they would have been sentenced to death, "and that public opinion would not now tolerate the sentence of death for rape." It goes on to say that "the idea of shutting mere lads in gaol for the rest of their lives is too monstrous to be contemplated."

Three prominent Sydney clergymen agreed with the *Herald*, and while noting that various clever dodges were at times used to avoid the full sentence, they said that as the law stood it prescribed the heavy sentences, and **to hope that such dodges would always succeed was not the way for society to work**. In any case, with the current case, no such dodges had yet been applied, and the youths stood sentenced to life.

Opinions flooded in, and inevitably spread to the discussion of why rapes occurred, and whether various forms of punishments and treatments would be effective.

Letters, Gordon Garner, St Andrews Presbyterian Church, Bexley. Sex education has been persistently suppressed within the NSW Education Department. For an adolescent who lacks an adequate sex education, the posters in our city are not so much informative as an incitement to lust. Certain newspapers feature the demi-nude daily to foster sales, and newsagents' shops are full of pornographic covers and writing. **I have yet to find the newsvendor who displays anything on sex education.** I do not wish to imply that a mere removal of these sexy productions would control sexual impulses any more than the hiding of knives would banish suicide.

The Crimes Act within NSW is an affront to people of intelligence and insight. It sinks below the law of talon with is rough justice of "eye for eye, tooth for tooth". An enlightened, forthright community should demand **psychotherapy until cure for its sex offenders, instead of a life sentence**.

One can only hope the prison reform committees, New Education Fellowship, Marriage Guidance Council of NSW, and the Father and Son Movement of our State will go on to create such a body of informed opinion that a generation will arise which will repeal our stupid Act or make it thoroughly dead through disuse.

Letters, John M O'Brien. One of the reasons for alarming increase in such cases is the so-called "humanitarian" attitude that is being adopted towards the perpetrators of these fiendish acts.

I fail to see that if previous generations saw it fit to institute the death penalty for rape, why that now, in 1954, proposals should be put forward to abolish it, along with life imprisonment. Has the crime lost any of its heinousness during the passing generations?

In my opinion, the only deterrent to these crimes **is savage reprisal by the law, by carrying out the death penalty.**

There were many other writers. For example, in brief:

Douglas Darby, MLA, concluded that whipping should be provided for extreme cases of calculated brutality.

Bessie Lundie thought that boys should be given an opportunity to rehabilitate themselves, and a suitable institution should be established for this purpose. They should not be thrown into prison with professional criminals to be further contaminated.

GMP asked what is going to be done with the four lads? Are they going to be put behind bars and given some work that may, or may not, be useful? Or are they going to be helped by psychiatrists, social workers, and Christian men of commonsense?

John Robson, Director of the Father and Son Welfare Movement, wrote that we can consider the depravity of offenders, condemn the education system, berate the Churches, and deplore the commercialisation of sex.

In so doing, we should remember that Herbert Hoover, head of the American FBI, declared that a society **in which**

divorce is the order of the day, premarital sex experience is so widespread, and there exists a general looseness in regard to the Christian moral standard, then the morals of the youth can hardly be expected to rise to a higher level.

NEWS AND VIEWS

Letters, S Timmins. As a property owner and ratepayer to the Water Board and to local government bodies, I cannot understand the Board as a whole deferring action on a recommendation for the tightening up of **the by-laws governing illegal plumbing**, which was submitted to it by its engineer-in-chief and by its president.

Mr A Moverley at the meeting is reported to have said: "Some people may run a pipe down their backyard, and although it's a breach, it's not serious."

As a licensed plumber, let me inform Mr Moverley that such a thing is serious. Whether it be a waterpipe or an underground waste pipe that he is referring to, it is breaking the law and should never be condoned.

The Government saw fit to license only two trades in the building industry – plumbers and electricians – because their work entailed a skill, which was necessary to save and preserve human life.

Unless the public is made aware of the dangers of illegal plumbing, and the Water Board, health authorities and local government bodies take this matter up seriously, and punish to the extreme any unlicensed person interfering with wastes, water or sewerage, and thereby perhaps spreading disease throughout the towns and cities, I feel that our expanding city will be faced one day with an epidemic due to illegal plumbing, which Mr Moverley and the Water Board seem to condone.

Letters, Property Owner. Having recently been charged 30 Pounds by a licensed plumber for one and half days' work, all materials being found by myself, I suggest that the Water Board give a little thought to property owners who have been pushed around for years by licensed plumbers .

Would it not be better if the board gave consideration to some scheme whereby property owners could be issued with a permit to carry out their own work instead of forcing them further into the grasping hands of licensees?

After all, any work carried out under a permit has to be passed by the board inspectors before it can be brought into operation, and surely if it is done to the satisfaction of such inspectors, does it matter who actually does the work?

It seems strange that the local council will issue me with a permit to build a house, yet I cannot get a permit from the MWS and D Board to even screw a tap into a pipe inside that house.

Kangaroos in packs of hundreds are bounding over vast areas of NSW **eating whatever greenery they can get**. This is because of the drought in wheat areas, and their devastation is beyond the capacity of graziers to control.

A toddler fell into **a hot copper** yesterday in a Sydney suburb while her mother was **boiling the clothes**. Despite efforts, the baby died.

JULY NEWS ITEMS

Donald Peers, British pop-song idol, is in Australia for a tour. You might remember him for his signature song **"I told them all about you."**

The Darts Association of NSW will be holding its fourth annual championships later this month. There are 8,000 players registered in darts clubs in Oz, and **about 12 million in England and Wales.**

The NSW Hospitals Commission has issued instructions that **hot-water bottles must no longer be used in public hospitals.** This is because they cause **scalding damage if they leak.** There is considerable opposition to this order by staff who claim that if you seal them properly, they do not leak. So why deny their comforts? **Instead just get staff to do their jobs properly.**

There is significant talk that **seven nations** will form a South East Asia Treaty Organisation, called **SEATO.** The countries are Australia, US, Britain, France, Philippines, New Zealand and Siam. **The US** had no territorial interest, **Britain** had Malaya, Singapore and Hong Kong, and **France** had Cambodia and Vietnam. **All very imperialistic, but the old empires were breaking up at a rapid rate.**

The Indo-China war had just been concluded with a pact (see later this Chapter). This means that the world is **without a war for the first time in 23 years.**

The Post Master General is responsible for **collection of fees for the licensing of radio receivers.** It reported that, in the last three months, **351 people had been prosecuted for not having a licence for their radios.**

Licensed grocers in Sydney are being fined for **selling beer in lots of less than a dozen.** Sales of single bottles, or half-dozens are illegal. Why is this? Who knows!

The Communists have conquered all of mainland China, and the previous National government of Chiang Kai Shek is holed up in the off-shore island of Formosa. The US, anti-Communist, is supporting Chiang. They forlornly hope he can stage a comeback, with their help...

The Reds on the mainland want to join the UN. The US is blocking this, saying that the Reds are not the legitimate rulers in China. Australia is supporting the US position. **Tempers here are flaring over this issue.**

In 1954, the postal services and the telephone were run by the one Department, the Post Master General. One of the services it offered was **a duplex phone service,** whereby one person shared his line with a neighbour, though both of you had the same number....

Complaints are growing. Teenage daughters are taking up too much time, and neighbours who have fallen out are leaving their phones off the hook. The idea was a good one **to help increase the number of houses with phones,** but it had **some practical problems**.

A train traveller wrote to the *SMH* saying that he had been a **long-distance journey** in Second Class, and that it was clean and comfortable, and the train was on time. **Remarkable.** No one ever writes when things go well.

THE PETROV AFFAIR

For the month of July, the circus came to Sydney. Dozens of legal entities, including three judges, attended a Royal Commission into the alleged spy ring run by Russian diplomat Petrov and his wife. The claim being investigated was that this couple had recruited Australians, by as yet unknown methods, and cajoled them into providing valuable information that was of use to the Russians in their quest to achieve something. What that something really was would doubtless become obvious as the Commission proceeded, but it seemed from the ominous reportings in the salacious Press, that it would be most dire and threatening to the security of this nation.

As it turned out though, the first four weeks revealed not very much. The Petrovs gave evidence, and the most startling fact was that Mrs Petrov tried at Embassy parties to get friendly with a few people who might be of use to them. Towards the end of the month, a Document J was talked about at length, and a few persons were named in it as collaborating with the Russians. But it was not clear who had written it, and whether it was indeed authentic. One journalist who might have known all about it refused to give evidence, but no action was taken to force answers from him.

As the month ended, the enquiry had found almost nothing of substance, despite the enthusiasm and exaggeration of the Press. Labor, through Doc Evatt, was slowly digging a big hole for itself. Still, he had ways of making that hole even deeper, and you can wait, confident in the knowledge that he will do so.

INTERNATIONAL AFFAIRS

The French in so-called IndoChina had been under military attack for the last seven years. In Cambodia, Vietnam and Thailand, the people were anxious to be released from the colonial rule of the French, and a patriotic movement to achieve this had joined together with local Communists to fight, in various ways, for independence. Gradually, the French accepted that they just had to surrender their power, and after a long period of fighting and diplomacy, a peace was agreed between all the interested parties in July. The war was over, and peace would now descend onto the peninsula. No doubt.

By the Agreement, Laos and Cambodia would become independent nations. In Vietnam, the situation was not so simple. The northern half of the nation would come under the undisputed control of the Communists. The southern half would be independent.

This treaty was not seen as satisfactory by many. It was reached mainly because the French were keen to avoid the expense of ongoing military operations there, and so they had accepted a half-baked solution. It seemed inevitable that, in future, the aggressive Communists to the north would not be contented to have a Capitalist state to their south, and that for opposite reasons, the US, paranoid about Communism, would look for chances to change the new set-up. Indeed, not so many years later, the north and south were at war, and China and the US, and Australia, all had thousands of troops dying there.

In Australia, the signing of the treaty caused considerable misgiving. It was said that the limits to Communism, formerly at the Chinese border, had now moved down halfway across Vietnam. The dreaded scenario of the Reds pushing ever southwards was again raised, and Tasmania was seen by some as perhaps the ultimate goal of world Communism.

WAR WITH BRITAIN

During WWII, normal sporting competitions between Australia and Britain were cancelled. That meant the temporary end to cricket, Rugby League and Rugby Union Test Series, previously played here every third or fourth year. By 1954, they were back to their normal pattern, and this year it was Australia's turn to host the Brits in Rugby League for three Tests.

The first two Tests and the provincial games had all been fairly civilised affairs. There were of course, the normal punch-ups on the field and off among the spectators, plenty of drinking off the field, and plenty of bad-mouthing and barracking. Again, on the field and off. All completely normal for Rugby League.

On 10th of July, a major match was played in Sydney, between NSW and the Brits. A big brawl broke out on the field, and the punch-ups lasted for five minutes, with the crowd of 27,000 all the while baying for blood. Official public reaction was strong and condemnatory. One clergyman called for the abandonment of the rest of the tour, and the Letters below show that this time, the violence had gone too far, and some re-thinking might be needed.

Letters, J W Wilson. After such a disgraceful brawl on the Sydney Cricket Ground last Saturday, the trustees of the ground should allow **Soccer football** more use of the No. 1 ground.

There seems to be more wrestling, punching and kicking than real football in Rugby League, and it is a shame that the Rugby League people should have so much of the say as to whom the ground should be allotted.

Soccer is correct football, and is gaining ground in popularity by leaps and bounds. Very soon Sydney is to have an international Soccer match, New Zealand v Australia. The Rugby League says it shall not be played on the Cricket Ground. This state of things should be altered.

Letters, Member. Good can come out of evil, and Saturday's fiasco at the Sydney Cricket Ground may lead to the trustees breaking the stranglehold which the Rugby League holds on that ground, and permit members to see more, and varied, amateur sports.

At present those members who do not like professionalism in football are getting very little satisfaction out of being ground members.

In these democratic days it is time that Cricket Ground members were given at least an annual meeting at which the affairs of the ground could be ventilated.

Letters, EHS. The very low standard of sportsmanship into which the professional game of Rugby League has fallen, and exemplified in Saturday's England v NSW match, calls for a change from most of our primary schools back to **the Rugby Union as played in the past.**

It is my duty to teach the fundamentals of Rugby League to lads learning to play their first games of football. So widely has the league cult of barge, bash and spot spread, that I find I have first of all to eliminate headlock and stiff-arm tackles, punching, kicking and tripping, and then teach that the game is the thing. The response is most encouraging and it is a pity this material has to backslide as it goes to the bigger fields of Rugby League.

The time has surely come for the Public Schools Amateur Athletic Association to throw off the grip of the professional league with its false values, and encourage a return to the amateur Rugby Union which plays hard football with a degree of true sportsmanship apparently unknown in league.

Letters, N Z Visitor. People get the Governments, and crowds get the footballers, which they deserve.

The trouble last Saturday was largely due to the spectators. The behaviour of the players did not shock me so much as the many anti-British comments I heard. If the Englishmen have been continually subjected to this vituperation on the slightest provocation, it is no wonder they have vented their resentment in the Australians opposing them.

Sydney people have become shockingly one-eyed about their League football; they take it too seriously. The current local idol would not come within cooee of a place in the Rugby Union All Blacks or the Springboks.

Letters, Disgusted. Congratulations to EHS for his splendid Letter on the subject of Rugby League football, and his bold stand against an organisation which apparently dictates to certain primary schools what game they should play.

I know that many other sports-masters would welcome the change proposed by EHS. Irrespective of what game the lads decide to play when they grow up, they would at least have been taught to play in a spirit which is gradually being divorced from the Rugby League.

I have been a member of the Cricket Ground for over 30 years but never have I witnessed on that or any other ground such a disgraceful scene as took place last Saturday. The display on the field was bad enough, but was matched by that made by a big proportion of the spectators, many of whom I am sorry to say were in the members' stand. I was also witness to a number of disgraceful scenes which took place adjacent to the English players' dressing-room, and I can only describe the atmosphere as putrid.

I feel that the Trust should be compelled now to offer some statement on what steps are being taken to preserve the dignity of membership.

Comment. The following Saturday, the Third Test was played. The players, to a man, doubtless chastened and threatened, behaved themselves perfectly, and the match proceeded in a tough but sportsmanlike manner. In support of the idea that it is **the game that counts and not the result,** I will not tell you who won this deciding Test.

WHAT CAN BE DONE TO STOP RAPE

Last month four boys were sentenced to life imprisonment for rape, and we looked at Letters that talked about the idea of mandatory sentencing. As that discussion matured, it turned more towards what might be done to prevent rape in the first place. Again there was a variety of suggestions.

Letters, Gerald Needs. I cannot agree that the death sentence for this offence in the case of those over age should be abolished. In my opinion, it should not only **be retained but enforced**.

To decent, good-living women, and I have heard many say so, **death itself is preferable to being raped**.

Whereas murder destroys the life of the body, in a woman, too often, rape utterly destroys her spirit.

The psychological case, although he may plead "irresistible impulse" still has his free will and knows full well what he is doing and the consequences of his act.

Our womenfolk need to be effectively protected against these degenerates and their protection should receive first consideration. The reformation of the criminal, if it is possible, is only of secondary importance.

Letters, Mrs E Stevenson. In view of the fact that so many women and children have been attacked in various suburbs by some sex fiend, it seems inexplicable that clergymen and others can be suggesting **lighter punishment for men convicted of the crime of rape.**

Would these people take such a lenient view of the matter if the victim happened to be their own daughter or wife?

It is not always possible for mothers to accompany children to and from school, so one has to try to instill a fear of all strange men into their hitherto trusting minds.

What anxiety a mother endures if her little girl is late in arriving home from school can be readily understood by all mothers.

Letters, Edward Baker. You show a decided preference to excuse the criminal rather than the sympathy that might reasonably be expected for the victims and their relatives.

These days, through the sentimentality of those who should know better, the criminal in Australia generally knows for a start that he can generally **get away with anything, by working the sob stuff.**

Letters, Phyllis Jackson, Women's Group, NSW Liberal Party. Recognising that individual social behavior has **its foundation in family training**, the committee believes that much juvenile delinquency and crime can be traced to defects in home life and in particular to the failure of parents adequately to discharge their responsibilities towards their children.

The committee feels that as a useful first deterrent, the community should endeavor to **sheet home to the parents** concerned their responsibility for the antisocial acts of their children. Accordingly, it feels that presiding magistrates and Judges should be empowered to instruct **the parents** of first and second offenders **to attend a series of lectures** to be given by leading sociologists. In addition, the existing ban on the newspaper reporting the juvenile cases might well be removed so that the full spotlight of publicity might be bought to bear.

The Liberal Party's women's group believes that the State Labor Government should have **set up an investigating committee** comprising sociologists, church leaders, educators, and members of the medical profession, to determine if reforms might be devised whereby the incidence of crime, and particularly crime against women and children might be radically reduced.

Letters, E Collocott. What is it that drives youths and young men into such wrong, cruel, and, one would think, unsatisfying, attacks? **They, too, are victims of something.** More important than punishment is thorough and far-reaching inquiry into the social and psychological sources of such behavior. Understanding is more difficult than moral indignation, or even pity, but infinitely more valuable. Such things are symptoms of wide social ill-health. We cannot discharge our social responsibility by merely hiding its victims, active or passive, in gaols.

Letters, 11 Womens Organisations. Sydney. We feel that wider discretionary powers should be vested in the Judge in such cases where they involve youths under the age of 18 years.

And this, not alone because of the mandatory severity of the penalties for rape in the present Act, but because the Judge is more competent to impose sentences and treatment better calculated to salvage whatever manhood still remains in the offenders before him.

If the Crimes Act is so amended and if the sentences imposed more in accordance with the public conscience, we might hope to stamp out the present undemocratic law-flouting practice of sentences being set aside by the Minister of Justice at the behest of pressure groups.

In our opinion, the incurable **sex pervert should be permanently** segregated in the interests of themselves and the community at large.

Is it not time, therefore, that the framers of our penal system should realise that our **sub-normal criminals should be separated from the normal**, and that vicious incurable cases should be permanently segregated, and that reformative methods should be regarded of greater importance that punitive, and that all the powerful agencies that go to the moulding of character should be pressed into the service of youth in a national scheme to salvage our boys and girls, from the depravity which is taking its revenge upon society in acts of horror and brutality.

Letters, R Byden, The Rectory, Milsons Point. The technical theological term is **Original Sin**, a tendency to evil innate in all men, and being in their case, seemingly, unchecked by religious faith, practice, or example, reaching this natural fruition via uninhibited self-indulgence.

All Churches are already doing much youth work, but **non-churchgoing, non-praying, non-religious parents are a major frustration.**

Cure of these evils is a spiritual matter, but effective contact with whole masses of modern paganised youth, especially that large section which is also crudely barbarous in background and outlook, is the really baffling problem.

Letters, J Weiss, Council for Child Advancement. My organisation is interested in the connection between **low grade reading material** available to our young people and delinquency.

We feel that the real causes of sex offences are social, and should be investigated by responsible bodies such as church and educational organisations.

Letters, F S Boorman. Youth to-day is increasingly exposed to the excitement and incitement of certain unsavoury literature and magazine covers so prominently displayed on counters; to newspaper articles and advertisements for films; to the immodest attire of some females on our beaches and elsewhere.

Our youth would **barely be normal if they grew up unaffected by such influences** as beset them through their adolescence. We should do something about such matters and give our children a chance. Then with our conscience clear, we could justifiably punish the evil-doer.

Comment. On the question of the efficacy of various forms of punishment, and the separate question of the causes of rapes, there was clearly no agreement among writers. There was a general agreement that mandatory death sentences should be abolished, though there were many who vigorously supported them. There were only a few writers who thought flogging would do the trick, but they were absolutely steadfast in their beliefs. There was a majority of later writers who were convinced that the parents and family should bear blame, and some who went so far as to say that the perpetrator was the victim of his upbringing. And so on. No matter what aspect was looked at, there was great division on it.

HOT WATER BOTTLES

Letters, Kiki Mathews. It seems rather absurd that the Hospitals Commission has issued an order that hot-water bottles must not be given to patients in public hospitals. Surely it is the doctor who is in charge of the individual patient who is to say whether that patient needs, or should have, hot-water bottles.

Letters, Jocely Henderson. As one who has used hot-water bags for many years, and knows their value when looking after invalids, I wish to know why the Hospitals Commission has forbidden their use in hospitals, even when there is no other alternative facility provided for continuous heating.

It is interesting that in your recent report of the ban, all the adverse comments came from hospitals run by the Commission in comparatively warm climates.

Letters, Desda P Capp. The order forbidding the use of hot-water bottles in hospitals is harsh treatment indeed for patients, particularly older people whose vitality through illness is lowered.

It must be remembered that patients are without exercise and often only able to take very little nourishment.

Letters, I S A. The danger from hot-water bags is caused by air seeking an outlet. This causes the bag to rip.

All air should be pressed out before screwing on the stopper and bags should not be filled to capacity.

They should be examined each time of using for the tiniest leak; few accidents would occur if this is done.

Letters, P McGaghey. My experience of hot-water bags is that they are not safe to use after the first winter. Each time we have used them in the second winter, they leak.

NEWS AND VIEWS

Motorists were upset because their insurance was rising all the time. **In earlier years, judges had decided** the compensation to be paid for injuries. **Now, however, juries made that decision**, and were accepting all sorts of sob-stories, and then **making big grants. "The insurance company can afford it".**

AUGUST NEWS ITEMS

A two-year-old Italian girl died in Stanthorpe Hospital (Brisbane) from **eating rat poison** from a tin she found near a rubbish dump.

News item, August 5th. "**Vice Squad police early today raided a house** in Palmer Street, East Sydney, and **arrested thirty men**. These men were charged with having been in a common gaming house this morning. It began shortly after mid-night when police smashed the door of the building down with a 16lb sledge hammer."

Gambling in the form of two-up and baccarat was a feature of Sydney night life, and of all Oz cities. Floating schools (different addresses every night) were very popular. **Police generally turned a blind eye**, except for the few raids every week.

The Archbishop of Canterbury, Dr Geoffrey Fisher, said that **of the world's Christians**, 52 per cent are Roman Catholics, 23 per cent belong to various Protestant bodies, 20 per cent are Orthodox, and 5 per cent Anglican.

The NSW Road Safety Council has suggested that **blood tests be used by police to test whether a person is under the influence of liquor**. The tests would be administered by a doctor, and the results admissible in court, and could also be used by the defence. A high reading **would not necessarily indicate that a person was incapable of driving**, but just give an indication of how much alcohol the person had consumed.

In New York, **an armless man has been charged at Chicago with forgery**. The man writes with a hook on the stub of his right hand, and he was charged with cashing four Government tax refund cheques.

Mrs Charles Jill, aged 42, of Hargrave Park, in Sydney, on Sunday, gave birth to **her 17th child**. She now has nine boys and eight girls. She also has five grandchildren.

The Treasurer, Sir Arthur Fadden, brought down the budget on August 18th. He said that the nation was more prosperous than at any time since the war, and so he would be **cutting income tax by an average of 12 per cent. Also sales tax will be cut** by about two per cent, and the **means test for pensions** would be eased a little. Excise on brandy, ice cream and other stuff would be reduced. **Can you believe it: Taxes going down**.

The **Wiltshire Common-cold Research Centre** in England said that it had made **no significant progress towards finding a cure**. The *SMH* said this was a "shocking disappointment", perhaps with its tongue in the cheek. The Centre, still cure-less, closed in 1989.

A nice little controversy erupted over **Pat Hills** in Sydney. He was currently the Lord Mayor of Sydney, and **also** the elected Member for Phillip, a safe Labor seat. Various unions were complaining because Hills was apparently breaking the union rule of "**one man, one job**", a rule that zealous unionists were keen to enforce. Hills replied that **as Lord Mayor he was not paid, and so he had only one job**. Lots of fur was flying all round.

THEATRES OPEN ON SUNDAYS?

Across the nation, the various States had different rules for Sunday entertainment. There were a few rules they had in common. No form of entertainment was to start till after church services were finished, that is about noon. Sunday sport was only just tolerated, and under no circumstances were professional sports allowed. For amateur sporting matches, no entrance fee was to be charged. Picture theatres were allowed in major cities, but the last session had to finish by 9pm. Public transport throughout Sunday was almost nil, so that it made a trip to see a movie all that much harder.

Sunday live theatre had received some government approval during the war. That was because servicemen on leave were prowling the cities, and it was thought wise to get them off the streets. So major cities licensed perhaps two theatres to each run a single show in the early evening, and smaller cities got one. These turned out to be very popular, especially with American servicemen, but after the war, the licences were revoked.

So by 1954, the cities were a wasteland on Sunday, and were almost dead. The churches were the main spokesmen for this, but they were well supported by much of the population who thought Sundays should remain sacred, and that the Sabbath day of rest was in the interests of families.

There were others, however, who voiced a different opinion.

Letters, Tim Foster. If the Churches can attract some people on Sundays, let them. If they can convince some people that they should stay at home on Sundays, good luck to them. But why do they insist that **everyone**

must do these unnatural pursuits all day on Sunday. They cannot claim the live theatres are corruptive influences. And turning to sports, surely they must acknowledge that the playing of sport is good for everyone who does it. Do they claim that the gate money collected on Sundays is different from any other money? It just goes to pay for the sports to continue.

The problem is that the wowsers in the Churches have got control of the Churches just like the active Communists have got control of the unions. In both cases, the policies they put forward are extreme and do not represent what the rank-and-file think.

I would like to see **every Church hold a ballot of members to see whether they do in fact oppose Sunday entertainment**, and then we would see if they really do.

Letters, Relax. As the State Government is going to hold a referendum on drinking hours, might I suggest that another question be added to the ballot paper: "Are you in favour of theatres and picture shows being opened after 12 noon on Sundays?"

If the Premier intends considering the drinking members of the community, he should take this opportunity of considering the lots of the lonely thousands in our growing metropolis living in rooms and elsewhere, who walk the silent streets on Sunday with nowhere to go.

The argument for the opening of theatres and picture shows after 12 noon on Sundays is now a strong one, and should not be ignored by the Government.

Sydney is the second city of the British Commonwealth; thousands are pouring into the State under the Commonwealth Government's heavy immigration programme, and thousands of Australians, experienced by travel, are used to the great relaxation of theatres and picture shows on Sundays.

If theatres are open in London, Paris, New York and all major world cities, as they are, the time has arrived for us to fall into line. If Church leaders overseas do not object, surely no objection can be raised here.

Letters, N Benton. Picture theatres are open on Sundays not only in London and other major cities, as "Relax" says, but in all the provincial towns of England.

The first performance is at 4.30, the second at about 7 o'clock (noon is too early because there are too many outdoor distractions during daylight on Sundays).

The unions do not object. Employees, of course, get penalty rates, and do not have to work on Sundays if they do not want to. From my inquiries while in England, I gathered there would be a very public uproar if any attempt was made by Sabbatarian or other interests to ban Sunday shows, which help to keep young people off the streets and out of the parks and generally lighten the gloom of this day.

Theatres are, rightly, not open. Actors must have one day off and they cannot be accommodated with an alternative week day as cinema employees can.

Letters, Gloomy Sunday. "Relax" seems puzzled as to why we cannot have a referendum on Sunday picture theatres.

The motion picture industry in Australia is a close preserve similar to the breweries, and what it says goes, regardless of the people's wishes. In order to open Sunday picture theatres, the managements would have to increase rates of pay for the Sunday holiday, and rather than give themselves the trouble they join with the over-pious in protesting against the screening of after-church films.

I agree on the dullness of an Australian Sunday, more especially for the adult who is lonely and the visitor from overseas. But, but there it is.

SAFETY DOORS FOR TRAINS.

Here's a novel idea. If you have an electric train, one thing you can do is **allow the passengers to open and shut the doors themselves**, and that means you can have passengers fall out of the moving train and be killed at will. Another thing you can do, is have the doors close automatically when the train is about to leave the station. The problem with this is that some people might get caught in the doorway for a second, but the clamps on the door can be made of soft rubber that allows such persons to pull free. **Just as they were currently doing on buses and trains round the world.**

When this matter was discussed by the NSW authorities in August, they decided that automatic doors imposed a bigger risk to human life than **the current toll of one person per month** being killed on Sydney's suburban trains. In making this decision, they were influenced by a recent event in Japan, where central controls on a carriage failed, so that people could not get out, and **were thus incinerated within their carriage**.

This was a serious matter, and it is easy to see how their decision was made. But there was another side to this, and it was put by the Letters given below.

Letters, Rob Doors. The Railway decision-makers need to re-consider. They need to remember that the last year has been extremely wet, so that the passengers have kept the doors closed most of the time. In a normal year, the doors would be mainly open, and probably 20 people, not 12, would fall to their deaths.

Then again, what are the chances that a Japanese-style incineration will occur? Surely they can make provision against this happening. Surely it will not cause more than twenty deaths a year.

Letters, F A Dawson. The case for automatic doors, irrespective of the gravely deliberated views of local politicians, has been indisputably established by a demonstration during the last quarter century in London. The object lesson is there in tangible form for any transport undertaking to study. All the numerous Australian visitors to London know of the superlative efficiency of the London Under-ground system, which is entirely equipped with automatic doors.

Amidst his pontifical, high sounding generalities about efforts for the safety of the public, the Minister made passing references to the London system and dismissed it on two points. He stated that London trains operate predominately underground, which is not, in fact, entirely true. London trains are submerged only in the city and cover a considerable mileage on the surface in the suburbs. But in any case, what is the significance of the remark? A man can fall out an open door equally easily in a tunnel or on the surface.

His second point was that the London climate is different. This is undoubtedly true, but I have yet to learn that the only known method of ventilating trains is to leave the doors open.

What Mr Wetherell seemed not to consider worthy to mention was the number of cases of accidental death on the London Underground and the number of occasions when its automatic doors have imprisoned accident victims. This information would, of course, have damned the local decision completely, because

such things don't happen on the London trains. All the doors, although operated by a master control for normal purposes, are fitted with emergency controls for individual operation. Moreover, a single person can push a door open manually with no great effort. Since every coach has eight doors, Londoners have no cause for alarm.

The apparently isolated case in Japan seized upon by our authorities is hardly a strong argument. Surely the day has yet to come when Western countries seek guidance from Japan in matters of engineering.

Letters, E Gordon-Hume. Mr Wetherell and Mr Winsor are apparently oblivious to the fact that our single decker buses have self closing doors.

SHIRLEY BEIGER

Earlier in August, a Sydney model was arrested and refused bail, for the shooting of a man. Apparently he had been at a nightclub in Sydney's Kings Cross with another woman, and she had seen him there. She had gone home, got a gun, and returned and shot and killed him. On August 23rd, she appeared in the NSW Supreme Court, applying again for bail.

Comment. This led to court cases that caused a sensation throughout the rest of the year. At this stage, I will not elaborate of the ultimate outcome, but will instead give you an introduction to the defence she would later produce. This defence is a statement she made to the Court about the night in question.

I came home from work and Arthur and Don were sitting in the flat talking. Arthur said he had to go to the dentist at quarter to six. He went on to Don's and

I heard him say to Don that he would see him down at work.

He put on his best suit and a silk shirt and tie. I knew then that he wasn't going to the dentist and I was hurt to think he had lied to me.

I had put the heater on and warmed all his clothes before he put them on, so he wouldn't be cold. I wanted to believe he was going to the dentist because I didn't want to know that he was lying to me....

Then he went and I started thinking. He had been going out until all hours so often of late, and when I asked him where he had been he would say, with the boys. I just had to be sure, so I went to see if he really had gone to the dentist and I couldn't find his car, so I went down to Chequers, and there I saw his car....

I went out to Coogee in a cab and asked my mother if she would come and sit with me in town as I wanted to see for myself if Arthur was with another girl.

We sat and waited, and I prayed that he would be by himself. But at 11 he walked down King Street with this girl.

I didn't know what to do, I felt sick to see the man who had been in bed with me only a few hours before, telling me he loved me, and wanted me to marry him when he came back from overseas. He had said how he would tell our children all about his trip and what he wanted them to be like. And there he was, walking arm-in-arm with another girl, and when he was finished with her he would come home to me.

I was just the girl who washed his clothes, cooked his food and ran after him doing all odd jobs – even cleaned his shoes so he could be nice for other girls...

Mummy and I walked off and left him, and when I arrived home I knew that no matter what he had done I still loved him and I wanted him back.

I went down and rang up and they said he had gone. I went back to the flat and waited while Mummy went back to see if he had gone, and when she came back and told me he was still there, I just wanted to see him....

I saw some guns in the corner and remembered Don had a gun, so I decided I would take it with me and tell him if he didn't come home with me I would shoot myself...

I was going to just fire the gun and frighten him, and I knew he would not leave me alone if he thought I would do anything silly.

Mummy went in and got him and when he came to the car he wanted to know what I wanted...

He put his head through the window and said he would be home later and gave me a push, the way he always does when we have had words and he knows that he has won.

I must still have been holding the gun because next thing he was lying on the ground covered in blood. They brought me to the station and they told me Arthur was dead.

I still can't believe as he was so alive this afternoon. I didn't want him hurt. I loved him too much to see him hurt but I guess he will never be hurt again, will he? I still love you. – **Shirley Beiger**."

Comment. This long statement would become significant as the court proceeded through to its surprising verdict, in due course.

THE PETROV CIRCUS

This was turning out to be a most entertaining affair. Since the Royal Commission had come to Sydney early in the month, the Sydney evening papers, the *Sun* and the *Mirror*, had played it up every day, and were able to find banner headlines to fit any occasion. Sensation after sensation was what they screamed, though the more sober judgement was that factually it was all really a bit of a yawn.

For August, most of the action revolved around so-called Document J. This many-page epistle named three persons who had handed confidential national-interest papers to the Russians. Controversially, the three persons were all employees of Dr Evatt in his Department. Sensation. Was this true? To answer it, the author of Document J had to be questioned. But who had written it? That is what the Commission tried to find out, all month. But it got nowhere.

It was an even bigger sensation because the Labor Party was always accused of being in bed with the Reds. Now here it might be that the staff of the Labor Party's leader was handing information to the Reds. What did this say about the linkage now?

Dr Evatt, much to the consternation of his Party, responded by saying that he would represent the three before the Commission. It could be seen that here he was, the leader of Labor, trying to protect his perhaps-spying minions from the long arm of the law. What was to be said about the linkages this time?

Evatt, in his fashion, went ahead regardless, and made matters worse by clashing regularly with the three Commissioners. Evatt was a distinguished jurist and had in earlier times occupied the highest legal position in the Land, as Chief Justice of the High Court. Now he was up against three judges of less rank than he had held, and he had none of the respect for them that they should expect when presiding over a Commission. So Evatt was always in hot water.

The Labor Party was in turmoil. Every week, some committee or other called for Evatt to give up his defence of the three, and even went so far as to suggest he resign as leader of the Party. But Evatt remained entrenched and the Party fulminated in vain.

The month ended with more and more people being convinced that the enquiry was just a circus. Many of them had ridiculed the idea that Australia had anything worth spying on, and now they were getting more certain in their views. Unless the Commission came up next month with proof that spies were active, and importantly that they were selling information that was of use to an enemy, then the idea that it was a joke, and that it was all put on to gain some political advantage, would be confirmed.

PRINCESS MARGARET UNDER PRESSURE

Princess Margaret at this time was in the middle of a difficult period. In 1953, she fell in love with a Court official, Peter Townsend, and he asked her to marry him. The problem was that he was divorced, and the Church of England and the Government said no to the union. She was told that she would lose her inheritance and income and status if she went ahead.

Skulduggery prevailed, and Townsend was shifted to a posting overseas, while Margaret was asked by the Queen to delay the final decision on marriage for a year. She was moved out of the country for months, and in the long run, in 1955, she issued a moving letter that said she would give up her marriage. Tough times for a beautiful young woman.

NEWS ITEMS AND TRIVIA

Raffles. You could not move without running into someone selling raffle and Art Union tickets. There were all sorts of good causes, the sellers were anxious to tell you. There was the local town band, the girls' vigaro team, the Catholic Churches building fund, the Protestant Churches Old Peoples' home, Legacy, the upcoming school fete, and the Police Boys Club. My eldest brother, and his greyhound syndicate, raffled a dog. It died before the raffle was drawn, so it was not a pleasant ending.

All of these were illegal and you were supposed to go to the State Chief Secretary's Department to get approval, but this took months and the answer was always negative, so they went ahead any way.

In any case, here is a note on the subject.

Letters, Helene Rankin, NSW Women Justices' Assn.
Surely one of the most important ways of preventing sexual attacks on children is to stop the young from roaming around the streets.

A serious breach of law is involved in very young pupils coming around, often at dusk, or during the evening, selling tickets for raffles, the proceeds to go to "providing sports equipment for the school."

Clause 23 of the Lotteries and Art Unions Act, 1901, states that "no person under the age of 17 years shall sell or offer for sale or be allowed to purchase a ticket

or take part whatever in connection with an art union
or the drawing of prizes in any Art Union.

NEWS AND VIEWS

General Motors Holden announced that it made a profit
of seven million Pounds during 1953. This was **by far the
highest profit earned by a public company trading in
Australia**. The profit was up 83 per cent from a year ago.

China is trying to join the United Nations. America will
not have a bar of it. On June 22nd, the UN again said "no"
to its attempt. This is the **170th time that China has been
rebuffed** from joining the UN or its agencies.

News item. Alice Springs, Sept 15th. **Aborigines here
have started to charge tourists for taking photos of them.**
A "black fella" will ask two Shillings for a snap of him
walking down the street, and that rises to five Shillings if he
stops and poses. For one Pound, he will take off his shirt,
and adopt a threatening pose with a spear or boomerang.
For a family group, the cost is thirty Shillings.

SEPTEMBER NEWS ITEMS

NSW will conduct a **referendum** on October 14th to decide the **closing times for hotels**. There will be a choice between 6pm and 10pm. **Licensed clubs will not be affected**, much to the relief of local RSL Clubs. **Beware, passions on display**.

In cities around Australia, it was becoming a popular pastime for persons arrested to **record the policeman's number** and soon after claim he was treated unjustly, and **often bashed**. The Papers were full of such claims, and **the Courts were filled with such actions**.

A Letter to the *SMH* applauded the new regulations proposing that the **cars of newly-licensed drivers** be adorned with a temporary plate **displaying the letter L.** This would indicate a **Learner driver**. He also proposed similar plates for a novice driver (N), and for **new cars being run in (R)**.

September 7th. The Sydney Coroner found that **Shirley Beiger** had killed a man called Arthur Griffith by shooting, and **sent her to trial for murder on November 15th**. She was refused bail. The Coronial enquiry was well attended, and each day about 50 people crammed into a Court supposed to hold just 30 persons.

American Dave Barry, **the man who does the roar at the start of MGM's films**, is in town for a short visit. He has been doing the roar for 17 years.

Could **Pat Hills** be a Member of the NSW Parliament, and at the same time continue as Lord Mayor of Sydney? Did this **violate the Union principle of "one man, one job"**? Well, the Labor Caucus met last night, and voted on this. They **ended up with 12 votes for and 12 votes against**. So it will probably go to the next meeting, when some absentees will have returned.

One Garrett Cashman at Albany in New York State flew yesterday for 90 minutes in a bucket suspended from 60 gas-filled balloons. He landed in a tomato patch after reaching a height of six thousand feet. **Police arrested him for flying without a licence.**

The Army announced on Sept 17th that it was now **reorganising for atomic warfare**. This was a grand statement in keeping with overseas countries, but in its details it said **nothing at all about atomic devices** or defences or weapons. Could it be, as one brave reporter said, "**all propaganda and hogwash**."

Comment. In the *SMH*, the heading over an item was **"Blackmarket for Tourists."** I wonder whether this would be **acceptable in today's world of extreme colour sensitivity**. Or, in fact, whether I can use the word "colour".

In the US, **the segregation of children** in the schools is a hot issue. In places like Virginia, white school after white school is **refusing to accept black students**, even though the Supreme court has said that this is unconstitutional.

COMICS

Colour comics are about to come to the Sunday papers. In a separate lift-out section, and sparkling rotogravure. No less. This will revolutionise Sunday reading, and the way the paper will be divided up among the family.

Comics were much more important then than they are today. The *Sunday Telegraph* had by far the best selection. Ginger Meggs, covering the front page of the Supplement, was a permanent fixture. Others, like Dagwood, came and went slowly. The *Telegraph* again was the winner **during the week**, with Joe Palooka on the back page, and Mandrake the Magician on the inside. Who can ever forget the wonderful way that Mandrake would gesture hypnotically to get out of trouble, with his giant Nubian slave, Lother, looming in the background? And what about his girl-friend, Narda. Yummy.

The *Herald* had to be content with lesser lights. Blondie was a spin-off from Dagwood, and was cute. Wally and the Major was actually sometimes funny. But between these two papers, and the two afternoon Sydney papers, they covered a big range, including Bluey and Curly. Cartoonists were also funny at the time, and were not the political satirists they have now developed into. I can remember one cartoon, from the great Emile Mercier, that showed a vast open golf course. In the forefront was a single post stuck in the ground, with a horizontal plank nailed to it. On it was painted "do not lean your golf-bags against this sign." Well…. I thought it was funny.

In this little world of make-believe, there were also **comic books.** Generally of 32-pages, they covered the same characters as above, and added saviours of the world like Buck Rogers and Hoppalong Cassidy. Then there were boys' **magazines** like the *Boys Champion*, and the *Girls Crystal* for the girls. Again 32 pages, these weeklies were from Britain, and were read and re-read over and over by children and teen-agers lying on their beds. No TV in those days in Oz.

I conclude this excursion into nostalgia, and away from the hard world of real things like terrorists and the Oz cricket team, with the thought that **I liked this world**. Not the poverty nor the ailments, nor the stifling of ideas and the narrow-mindedness, and so on. But just that bit of it that allowed young people some time to sit and read really stupid stuff, without all the crassness and commercialism and violence that confronts many of them in their leisure now, and that, sadly, they think is the only way to go.

TEACHERS AND COMMUNISM

The Acting Education Minister in NSW gained himself some headlines by warning teachers that some children in some schools were being indoctrinated by Communist "foreign parasites" to follow their philosophies, with the hope of gaining them as active members of the Party in the future.

A Mr Jones, of Sydney, doubted that this was true, and said it was an unwarranted slur on teachers to suggest that any of them would be guilty of this. He went on to say that:

Letters, K W Jones. One feels confident that the ill-considered remarks made by Mr McGrath, Acting Minister for Education, at the annual conference of the

NSW Teachers' Federation, will earn the same censure from the public as a whole as from teachers.

If, in his period of office as Acting Minister, Mr McGrath has found any positive evidence of indoctrination of children by "foreign parasites," why has it not been brought to light and the offender dealt with by the various means at the Acting Minister's disposal?

If on the other hand, Mr McGrath was not speaking from tangible evidence either of individual cases, of "warping and twisting" of children's outlooks or of political indoctrination in general, his remarks are calculated to do only harm in many different directions.

There are two effective instruments for the combating of Communism (or any other totalitarian ideology) open to our educational system. First, we must teach our children to think for themselves, to question everything and to reject that which does not recognise the timeless right of the individual. Secondly, we must win the confidence of our educators, believe in their integrity and recognise their worth so that they, in turn, realise their duties and regard our way of life as an honour to teach and uphold.

Letters, Marcia Kirsten. Mr McGrath is to be well applauded for his attack on these teachers who, by their example, encourage children in schools to regard Russian Communism as a mere political party doctrine separated from other party doctrines by a gulf no wider than that between our local Labor and Liberal parties.

My experience of teaching in State High schools and in private schools in this and other States in recent years has shown me plainly that many teachers of history and economics make their own personal views so plain that, young people by nature imitative, their pupils adopt these views as their own. Obviously no teacher openly advocates the Russian Communist system, but many teachers of my personal acquaintance sow seeds of distrust of our own national institutions.

No parent cares whether a teacher belongs to the Labor or to the Liberal party. No parent fears for its child's physical health if its teacher suffers from a cold. They do care if the teacher suffers from tuberculosis or smallpox. Even if contracted in a mild form, a major disease constitutes a danger to the community.

Letters, E Lawson. No clearer proof could be found of the extent to which a malevolently active minority of Communists has swayed the judgment of teachers that the outburst which followed Mr McGrath's speech to the federation.

Even the vast majority of moderates has become so habituated to Communist perversion of the concepts of freedom and solidarity that the attack on Mr McGrath passed almost unchallenged. Far from reflecting on teachers as a whole, the Acting Minister frankly and courageously condemned the Red minority. That minority has been busily warping the minds and distorting the outlook of pupils and fellow-teachers during the past 20 years, to my knowledge.

Here are some facts: The actual names involved are in the possession of certain teachers as well as myself and can be given to the Minister if he wishes:

A Communist cell in Newcastle, typical of those in all chief centres, included several male High school teachers. These had the task of "converting" a list of people in key positions, including any W E A, or university tutorial lecturers who were not already Communists. I learned most of the details of the procedure owing to the fact that I was a High School teacher, a university tutorial lecturer, and had some experience of public speaking. Hence I was in the "conversion list." As the Comrades thought I was certain to be roped in, they spoke of their aims and methods with engaging frankness.

It was part of the policy to get as many teachers as possible of English, history or economics to embrace Communism so that they could teach these subjects "from the correct slant." It was regretted that one active member was merely a teacher of mathematics, a subject rather difficult to paint red.

Communist teachers tried to get charge of High School libraries. Here they were to see that the sections dealing with history and economics contained plenty of Communist propaganda and they had also, unobtrusively and tactfully, to see that intelligent and adaptable pupils were encouraged to read the propaganda.

In some cases, there was a follow-up after promising pupils had left to take up careers such as journalism. Communists were told to infiltrate National Fitness camps and Boy Scout movements.

Some years ago, when the Teachers' Federation was Communist-controlled, their leaders pressed for a small, select Education Commission to replace management by the Public Service Board. Since the stability and conservatism of the Board made it impossible for the Communists to dominate it, they sought for the type of commission where Federation nominees would have more power. Even at the present session of the Federation this matter was brought up again.

While we are fighting to prevent Communists from betraying our national defence projects, we should congratulate Mr McGrath for denouncing those who would betray the nation more insidiously and more effectively by corrupting the minds and souls of Australia's children.

Comment. There was no doubt that Australia's Reds were working hard to gain supporters, and I have no doubt that a few of them pursued the tactics suggested in the above Letter. It seems to me though that they were not at all successful in getting converts, either in schools, or unions, or elsewhere. Granted in unions, the workers did follow them in union matters, and hoped to better themselves by their strikes and by playing difficult. But the Communists rarely managed to take seats at any elections at the national and State level, and I suggest that their deliberate attempts to manipulate were largely in vain.

JOHNNY RAY IN PERSON

Since the War, Australia had taken more notice of the US in all things, including a vast swing towards the appreciation of American music. Pop songs and hit parades and teenage adulation of so-called singers was a disease that swept the nation.

More and more US stars were making their way here for tours in Australia, and then in this month, the biggest name of them all (for a month) paid us a visit. It was Johnny Ray, and he had come for only three concerts. As you would expect when such a luminary arrived here, he was mobbed at the airport. His concerts were a huge sell-out, and hundreds of screaming teenage girls went beserk at them. He put on a performance that was full of gyrations never seen before (though now common), and sang and sang until he reached his signature tune, "**CRY**".

This song was his own creation, and was very popular at the time, probably because its message was so profound. I present a precis of it below so you can judge for yourself just how profound it was.

It tells of a person, presumably the singer, feeling a bit sorry for himself, and going for a walk. He sees a small talking cloud, that says it also has problems, it is well to recall that the sun will always shine. He asks the singer to remember him, "the little white cloud that sat right down and cried".

The last word was the focus of the song, and was uttered in a loud scream by Johhny Ray, in his high-pitched voice that increased the impact.

Now that you are duly impressed, I will give you some idea of the excitement he brought to Sydney. Below is an extract describing his escape from the crowds of worshipers.

Press report. Capacity houses of more than 15,000 each attended the two shows, at 6 pm and 9 pm. At least 200 people were jammed in the ramp leading up to the bleachers without a chance of getting of getting up to a seat for which they had paid seven Shillings each. A turnstile employee on the bleacher section said "Dozens of people have left and demanded their money back. It was the same at the earlier session."

One woman who said she had been in show business herself asked the police to take action to have her money refunded. She said that inside the bleacher section children and young girls were crying because they could not see the show. The woman worked herself into a frenzy. Eventually an official offered her money back. She told him she was "disgusted" and he could keep it to buy himself a taxi home.

Scalpers were getting up to £3 each for 30/ tickets for the second performance. One man who sold his ticket at a profit walked straight to the booking office window and bought two more at the correct price for the final show to be held to-night.

The promoters used a subterfuge to get Johnnie Ray out of the Stadium after his first show. A hire car with a police-man alongside it was parked outside the Stadium, and this was the one Ray and his entourage entered. Two motor-cycle policemen escorted this car and at a signal the Stadium gates were thrown open and Ray's car with the police escort sped out through the nonplussed crowd and back to Ray's hotel.

When the crowd from the first session swarmed out among the crowd waiting for the second, a huge traffic jam developed. Thirty extra police on duty diverted the traffic away from New South Head Road, and normal conditions were restored within half an hour.

When Johnnie Ray appeared the crowd went wild and pressed towards the entrance. Police were helpless for a while. They fought their way to a car. Police motor cyclists cleared a way through the crowd. Police clung to the running board of the car until it forced its way through the crowd and drove up Neild Avenue.

Comment. It all really was a great deal of fun, and the talented entertainer brought with him **a new era of audience participation.**

EVATT RIDES AGAIN: EVEN FURTHER

Dr Evatt's stage show continued. There was no doubt that by now he was the star, had the main role, was the most conspicuous actor, and certainly was the biggest prima donna. Let me flick through some of his grand scenes for the month of September.

Let me remind you about Document J. It was written by an unknown author, and given to our ASIO by the Petrovs.

No one knew who wrote it, and whether the information in it was true, or not. It named two or three of Evatt's staffers as spies. So Evatt appeared as advocate before the Commission to defend their integrity.

Evatt started to get paranoid about this. Or he masterly pretended to. In any case, he gradually, day by day, came publicly to the conclusion that the whole Petrov affair was simply an attempt to **get** him. **He was the intended victim**, and the whole thing was being manipulated to accuse him and the Labor Party of affiliations with Communists. He reasoned that Document J was a fake. Why had his staffers been named in it? Surely, it was just to defame him. Where had the document come from? The Petrovs. But they were known spies, and they had accepted bribes from ASIO and indemnity from the government to give evidence. Surely, if a document was forged, and if it was handed over to ASIO by the Petrovs, it was reasonable to assume that it came from conspirators who were out to get him. No suggestion was made that it was the **Government** doing this, but he left no doubt.

So he gradually pressed this case as the days wore on. Then, after a week, he got a chance to escalate his claims. The Commission revealed that in its earliest sessions, that were not public, it had heard (from the Petrovs) that a Mrs Ollier had told the Reds in Russia that a particular ship leaving Australia was carting ammunition for IndoChina. The French Government was alerted to this by ASIO, and they moved Mrs Ollier from their Embassy in Sydney, and she was ultimately arrested and was currently on her way to France.

Evatt sprang to the defence of the woman, and amid much posturing about conspiracies against him, sent urgent messages to the French demanding a fair examination of the case. The French Government sent stiff replies indicating that it was their normal practice to give **only** fair examination of matters, and that they did not need any urging from Evatt in order to do so.

At last the three Commissioners could stand it no more, and held a two-hour session in private. When they emerged, they announced that they had withdrawn Evatt's permission to appear before them. **He had been given the boot.**

Nothing daunted, he kept on and on. By the middle of the month, realising he was getting nowhere with his conspiracy theory, he dropped it. Later he announced that he would re-apply to be allowed to appear again and at the same time he demanded that the number of Commissioners be increased to five, and the Commission be given new rules of procedure.

At the end of the month, the judges said that they would go into recess for a time to allow them to consider the material they had gathered. By now, everyone welcomed this period of review, because the Evatt circus had distracted attention away from the original purpose of the enquiry.

So, a few sleep-ins were on the agenda for the judges, but sadly for them and the Commission, Evatt was still not finished. His biggest blue was yet to come.

Comment. Menzies had never said a word about the spying, nor the conduct of Evatt, nor anyone else. He kept a mile away from it all. Whether or not you like the man, there was no doubt that he was an astute politician. Evatt was destroying himself, while **he** watched at a discreet distance, with no apparent involvement at all.

NEWS AND VIEWS

Razor blades. I know you have been waiting for this. At last, **a discussion on razor blades**. These are not the cut-throat blades that were common prior to the War, which were single-sided and about three inches in length. Rather, they were the type used in so-called **safety** razors, double-sided, and made by Gillette I seem to remember. Electric razors were far away in the future.

Letters, L Anderson. Why is it that packets of razor blades produced by leading and lesser-known manufacturers, contain a high proportion of blunt and unusable blades?

The standard of blade seems to have deteriorated. Most men to whom I speak share my contention that it is rare these days to find one really sharp edged blade in a packet of five, or even a packet of 10. Formerly, one could expect four to five shaves from a blade. Nowadays (particularly within the last 12 months) it is possible to have only one and sometimes two smooth shaves from a blade.

Letters, E W. One simple and reliable way of restoring keenness to a dull safety-razor blade is to immerse it for five or six seconds in household ammonia and then wipe it dry.

Letters, M M. There is a relationship between a man's vitality and the toughness of his beard. Your correspondents should not over-look the possibility that they may be confusing cause with effect, and that their beards may be getting tougher. I am 78, and the blade I put in last February is not cutting as it should, but I am not sure whether my beard is getting tougher or the blade blunter. I think perhaps I should put in another blade.

Letters, Sheffield Steel. The trouble with many safety-razor blades now on the market is that they are too thin to hold an edge.

I have used Sheffield blades of the same make for over 20 years and find them reliable. My present blade has been in use since Easter seven days a week. After each use the blade is turned and after four days' use rubbed up on a glass tumbler and the edge is restored.

Letters, E McKenzie. May I mention that anyone who has used fine cutting tools for etching or engraving knows how metal tires and should be laid down occasionally to rest. It is the same with razor blades. Put used blades into a match box for say a month, then give them another turn. Still further use may be made of them by double-banking, i.e. putting two blades in the holder.

By these means a collection of say 30 blades may be made to serve indefinitely. It takes a little longer perhaps but is worth a try-out.

OCTOBER NEWS ITEMS

A Kings Cross movie theatre will **show movies on a Sunday**, starting at noon and they will rerun continuously till early evening. **No charge will be made for attendance**, though patrons will be given the **opportunity to make a contribution if they wish....**

The NSW Council of Churches opposes the suggestion because it **is not in keeping with the spirit of Sunday**, which should be a day of reflection, rest and worship. Methodists **disagreed with the proposal entirely**. A Roman Catholic spokesman said **that so long as provision is made for a person's religious duties**, there is no reason why that person should not have reasonable recreation facilities.

The Labor Party was in turmoil as the endeavours of **Dr Evatt** caused divisions among its members. NSW and Victoria State Branches were likely to move to at least censure Evatt, and **the rank-and-file were divided over him**. The Federal Secretary of the Labor Party summed it up when he described "some Labor men as either political pigmies, noisy nincompoops, loud-mouth limelighters or self-serving saboteurs."

NSW remains the only place in the British Commonwealth where insanity is not grounds for divorce.

October 26th . The State Cabinet decided yesterday **to abolish capital punishment in NSW**. The Cabinet acknowledged that **recently the death sentence has always been commuted to life imprisonment,** but while it was still on the books, NSW **was open to criticism as inhumane**.

The Labor Party was going from bad to worse. Apart from the disruption caused by Dr Evatt, it was split in some States, particularly Victoria, **by the presence of a Catholic faction that was determined to see all Communist influence removed from the Party. This Catholic Action faction** was well organised, and its presence was anathema to the left wing. Overall, the party was in strife.

It was getting popular to see **flying saucers**. A crowd of 15,000 at a soccer match in Florence in Italy on Saturday was in no doubt that it **saw saucers for 30 minutes**.

Hollywood movie star and much-loved comedian, **Charlie Chaplin,** had moved to Switzerland a few years ago because he was supposedly a Communist. He wasn't, he was just a bit left wing. Still, at the tail-end of the McCarthy era, the accusation was enough to damn him in USA….

The Russians sought to somehow gain political capital from exploiting this situation, so they offered him a high honour of the State, an award from **their World Peace Council, and this carried a large pot of gold with it**. When he came back from Russia, he offered some of the loot to a prominent clergyman, working for the poor….

The Abbe initially refused it. **"People will say I am serving Red soup to the poor. Can I as a Christian accept Communist money?"** After a few days of well-publicised delay, he found that he could.

DRINK AND BE DAMNED?

Next month, a NSW referendum will be held on the time at which watering holes should close each day. With the pubs, there was a clear-cut decision to be made. Either at six in the evening or at 10. With the fast-growing number of clubs, it was more complicated because it had first to be decided whether they should be included in the referendum.

At the moment, they were allowed to close at virtually any time they ran out of patrons. Such regulations that existed to limit their hours were almost always ignored, and the policing of them was a joke. So the clubs wanted to stay out of the referendum. The breweries wanted the same thing, because they sold a lot more grog that way. But the forces of temperance wanted all outlets to be closed at six, and many wanted them closed all the time. In the middle were the moderates, and about half wanted six, and the others wanted ten.

Over the last two months, a battle had been fought over whether the clubs should be included. As you saw through my monthly News Items, the pendulum swung back and forth, and it now looks like the clubs will be included. We will hear more of this next month. I point out that similar battles to this were going on in all States at this time, except for Tasmania and Queensland which already had more relaxed laws.

Seemingly in preparation for the highly-charged battle that was certain to come, the question of abstinence popped up on society's agenda for a few weeks.

It started with an innocent looking letter from a Mr Davies, and that brought forth a whole swag of Letters.

Letters, M B Davies. I would like to bring to your notice the invidious system of teaching health and hygiene in many of our Public schools.

A book, erroneously entitled "Health and Temperance Manual," and compiled by the **NSW Band of Hope**, is being used for the instruction of our children in matters of health and hygiene. The real title of this book should be "Health and Abstinence Manual," because that is what it teaches.

I firmly believe in moderation in all things, and my wife and I enjoy the occasional cigarette and drink. Now our son comes home and is firmly convinced that we have condemned ourselves in the sight of God and man because we have imbibed alcohol and nicotine. I consider this attitude to be an insult to my intelligence besides tending to breed into the child a feeling of insecurity and uncertainty as to the moral fibre of his parents.

Upon making inquiries, I am informed that no child is compelled to attend health and temperance classes in this State, but I am also told that my son would have to spend the duration of these lessons left to his own devices since no teacher could be spared to instruct him separately. This I can readily appreciate, but the fact remains that I consider health and hygiene a most important subject.

Surely it is time for the Department of Education (which openly recommends this narrow-minded book) to endeavor to give our children a full and comprehensive health grounding without pandering so much to the followers of total abstinence.

Letters, A. M B Davies's letter reminds me of a painful period in my life 30 years ago. I was then a London schoolgirl of 14 and as a Girl Guide I had for some time been exhorted (a) to obey and respect my parents and (b) that drink was a dreadful curse.

Our Guide meetings took place on a Friday each week and that was the day when my father brought home the microscopic wage on which he supported his large family. It was also the day on which my parents had their weekly treat – a pint of ale, costing 6d, for my father, and half a pint of porter, costing 4d, for my mother. As soon as I arrived home from the Guide meeting I was sent to obtain these beverages at the local off-licence – a place which could sell alcohol on draught but where no drinking on the premises was allowed.

How I hated this! I regarded my parents' one hard-earned relaxation of the week as exceedingly sinful and loathsome, and bitter words often passed between us before I departed on my unwilling errand. I can smile at the recollection of my priggishness now, but the pain and feeling of degradation which I experienced was very real – and quite unnecessary.

Letters, W M Hiley. I believe that the Education Department's approach to this matter is the one most calculated to improve the moral standard and social habits of the community and is deserving of the support and approval of all parents with a sense of responsibility.

While much evil may result from the questionable doctrine of "moderation in the use of all things" the teaching of total abstinence from alcoholic liquor can certainly do no harm and may do much good.

Letters, H Pick. Any child of average intelligence will understand, when it is clearly explained by parents, that an occasional drink or cigarette is by no means harmful. This is a far better and simpler way than excluding a child from health lessons altogether, as Mr

Davies suggests. I am convinced that a child would feel most uneasy if excluded, probably the only one in his class.

Letters, Gloster S Udy. When we consider the appalling effect of alcohol in personal and social life, then it's high time a few more children began educating their parents to appreciate that there is not one good thing to be said in favour of drinking alcoholic beverages.

Letters, Allen Garrett, Youth Temperance Council and Band of Hope Union of NSW. As an organisation with a Christian foundation, we are fully alive to the wide implication of the virtue of temperance, with its demands for self-mastery and self-control in every sphere and activity of life.

This does not deter us from our obligation to give the rising generation factual education about the nature and effects of alcohol, and the value of sobriety which the use of alcohol imperils. Indeed, one of the many reasons for such teaching is that intoxicating liquors so often weaken in young persons, modesty and moral self-control. To allow our children to become teenagers without having had an opportunity to learn from the competent and reasonable teachers of our Department of Education what authoritative scientists have to say about this narcotic drug, is to deny them a primary ethical right.

Admittedly it is far from wise to name **such men as Hitler and Stalin as examples of total abstainers**, and steps will be taken to eliminate such references in future issues of our handbook.

This leads me to assert that my organisation is cognisant of the fact that "teetotalism" alone will not save the world. We do believe, however, that the solution of the drink problem, which alas involves far more than drunkenness, will considerably simplify many of our other grave problems and will help advance the Kingdom of God on earth. We also believe that in the final analysis the one proven solution to this problem is personal total abstinence.

Comment. Whether or not I agree with the Band of Hope's philosophy, it is easy to agree with their opinion that it is not wise at all to cite Hitler and Stalin as exemplars of abstinence. **In fact, it is rather funny.**

Letters, Frank E French. The Band of Hope made me aware that my mother and father were really awful people. I was convinced they had hob-nailed livers such as were pictured on the walls of the B of H rooms in the most gorgeous sunset reds, greens, and yellows.

Another picture depicted snakes crawling in human bodies, and another was of a haggard, poorly clad woman nursing a starved-looking child. She was sitting by a dying fire. We sang doleful hymns and admonitions to father to come home – the clock has struck one and you know that you promised to come home as soon as your day's work was done. We feared that one day we'd get back home to find our mothers and fathers in some such condition – horrible thoughts to put into young and naturally loving hearts, and hardly calculated to strengthen the faith we had in our parents.

My mother lived to be a dear old lady, full of kindness to all about her and able to enjoy the beautiful things of life up to the day of her death at 96. My father had drunk wine or any other alcoholic liquor he desired every day of his adult life and might have reached a ripe old age, but a cab knocked him down when he was 88 and he lasted but another year or so.

I raise my glass in all sincerity and wish all total abstainers good luck. May they live to achieve for themselves freedom from intolerance which is at the bottom of this world's strife, and come to know the real meaning of temperance.

Letters, R. The most distasteful aspect of the matter is that every parent with a child at a State school must allow that child to be given instruction in the Band of Hope's version of health and temperance.

It is the duty of parents and educationists to equip children to take their place in society, which does not consist, in the main, either of drunkards or total abstainers.

I would like the Department of Education publicly to make known whether it intends to stand by its present ruling (thereby condemning itself as bigoted in favour of total abstinence), or whether it will widen the scope of its health teaching to conform to the views of the vast majority of the parents of this State.

Letters, R E Tebbutt. Even those who hold a brief for the liquor traffic would have to admit that alcohol is the greatest single source of evil in the community. All those who drink excessively were once moderate drinkers.

Why, then, inculcate into children the idea of moderate drinking? Surely the fewer of our children who learn to drink the better.

Comment. As a sure sign that the Letters were still coming in, the Editor of the *SMH* **closed correspondence** on this subject, after the last Letter above.

DIRTY DANCING IN CHURCH HALLS

Here we are fresh from instructions of how to save our children from the depravity of Grog. But there is no way we can relax. Now we need to be wary of the depravity of dancing in church halls.

Once again, a controversy was started by an innocent question that drew a huge response.

Letters, Anglican Communicant. Why is ballroom dancing discouraged or forbidden by some Church of England authorities in the Sydney Diocese?

Church-going parents in Sydney Diocese are at a loss to understand why the Church prevents their children from having dancing under the guidance of the Church, when there is nothing in the Church of England ordinance forbidding such social activity, which has always been part of the British way of life, and to which our beloved Queen gives her patronage.

Letters, C M Statham. The deplorable fact is that for generations our Anglican "authorities" have been obsessed by the view that the frostbitten rules of the puritan are none other than the ethics of the Christ. And they're not.

The result of the dominant influence of the puritan view of life in the Sydney Diocese has been disastrous – the loss to the Anglican fellowship of very many splendid people, especially young people. They've been frozen out, and I am not surprised.

The C of E here is in desperate need of rebels. Rebels, specially, in the ranks of the younger clergy, but also from among the laity. It is high time that someone hoisted the banner of revolt. I'm convinced that many very fine people would flock to it.

Letters, D Knox, Moore College, Newtown. Opinion is divided on the question whether or not modern close dancing is a hindrance to Christian living.

There are many in all denominations who agree with the "Catholic Encyclopaedia" that "round dances (i.e. waltzes), though they may possibly be carried on with decorum and modesty, are regarded by moralists as fraught, by their very nature, with the greatest danger to morals."

The majority of Church of England people in Sydney are of this opinion also, and they have expressed their wish that Church premises should not be occupied with dancing.

Letters, Another Anglican. I think that if all Churches suppressed gossip with the same burning ardour with which they suppress dancing, they would regain the confidence of decent fun-loving people.

Letters, M McDonald. As a mother and a practicing Anglican Churchwoman I am puzzled about one small aspect of this controversy.

Dr Knox and those who support him speak about the "danger to morals" involved in dancing in parish halls. Perhaps I am naïve; but I do wish they could be more explicit and explain what they mean.

I have attended occasional parish dances in the diocese of Sydney since I was a young girl, and I cannot imagine what dangers to morality could have existed at these affairs.

What Dr Knox calls "the mind of synod" is pleasantly disregarded by every Anglican school in the diocese. All of them, whether for boys or girls, hold dancing instruction, and most of them hold dances.

Letters, (Rev) Ken Short. He wants us to rebel against the "frostbitten rules of the puritan" which "dominate life in the Sydney Diocese." This naturally reflects upon those in charge of the diocese, and especially upon our Archbishop. May I draw his attention to the following facts.

I, at ordination, swore to obey (not rebel against) my ordinary. It is about time that all oaths taken before God were viewed seriously.

It is a fact that most of the young people in the Sydney Diocese who are interested in advocating dancing in church halls certainly find no place for Christ to be Lord of their lives.

May I humbly ask him the reason for the Church's existence. Is it to feed the sheep (as Christ commanded) or amuse the goats (as so many others desire)?

Letters, (Rev) H R Smith. To say that "young people will dance whether we like it or not" is a generalisation which is not completely true. But this is far from being a reason why the Church should follow the fashion of the world.

One could almost imagine the time coming when we will be called upon to encourage the art of "civilised" drinking to save our young people from the atmosphere of the public house.

MY ENCOUNTER WITH BOB MENZIES

About this time I was at the University of Sydney doing my under-grad degree. I was there on a Commonwealth Scholarship that paid my fees, and gave me enough money to live on for the university year. Perhaps I should have been thankful to the Australian taxpayer for their largesse, but such thoughts did not cross my mind.

Bob Menzies was coming to visit the Uni, and my football team knew the route he would walk. We wanted to make the point that our leather shoes had worn out and that we did not have the money to get them half-soled. If it had been Dr Evatt, or his deputy Arthur Calwell, we would have bunched up on him and shouted slogans. But, Bob Menzies commanded much more respect, so we decided to be more subtle.

We sat in a lounge that he would pass through, and arranged the furniture so that he could see the soles of our elevated shoes, resting on high divans. We thought that if he saw the plight of these 15 poor miserable shoe-damaged students, he would increase the student allowances. That was as subtle as we could get.

Bob came slowly into our room, talking and looking. He saw the soles of our shoes and immediately knew what we were doing. He stopped for a second, grinned just a little, and ambled on. At the doorway, he turned back a few degrees, raised his hand, and gave a half-wave and half salute, and went on. The team were by this time on their feet, and were so charmed by the majesty of the man that we clapped and half-cheered him. Then we went across to the Mays Family Hotel and drank our shoe-money.

Sixty years later, whenever my old football team gets together, we talk about this event. To a man, we all have a soft spot now for Menzies, no matter what we think of his politics. We forgive him for not raising our allowance.

NEWS AND VIEWS

Letters, W Bluett. The Minister for Agriculture, Mr E H Graham, has been asked to declare wild pigs "noxious animals," the object being to compel their destruction all over the State.

Don't let us become hysterical over this. There's another side. These wild pigs have their uses. They are on the Monaro country, industrious cultivators, aerating the soil and promoting the growth of good grasses. Their meat can be excellent, providing the animal is in reasonably good condition and of the "porker" age.

Above all, their suckers, if caught early, soon settle down in the sty and fatten readily. Because wild-bred ones have a long snout that is no detriment to their pork or bacon.

Grown wild pig, out of condition, may not be so alluring on the dinner plate as the sty-fattened. But when a man cannot afford patent leather shoes he contents himself with bluchers.

The increasing numbers we have now of New Australians feel the loss of pig meats in their accustomed diet. Isn't it sound economy to use the bush pork, now going to waste, to meet this demand? The meat may be tough – probably approved by dentists – but it is wholesome.

Surely the Australian Pig Society has more confidence in its product and has fairer ways of meeting competition than in demanding the immediate annihilation of a poor relation, whose one defect is toughness.

Letters, RSL Member. British servicemen suffered fully as much from the brutality of the Japanese war lords as did our men, and the Americans perhaps suffered even more, but today the Japanese Prime Minister is making an official visit to England and has been received in audience by her Majesty the Queen. In America, Japanese have been, for a long time now, welcomed as friends, and many sports teams have been invited as guests.

For years our own Servicemen have fraternised with the Japanese in their homeland, and many of them have married Japanese women, who have been received without hostility in Australia.

The plain fact is that although Japanese standards of warfare may not have been our own, Japan as a nation is no worse and no better than other nations.

For instance, the Germans and the Russians were equally as cruel and brutal, but does Mr Yeo suggest we should regard with hatred and bitterness all peoples who in the past have committed atrocities in time of war? If so, Australia will be almost alone and without support in a very dangerous world.

Comment. This voice of moderation was a sensible one, though there were still hordes of citizens who would not hear it. It was years and indeed decades before the bulk of the people were prepared to forgive and forget the threat and the misery created by the Japs in WWII.

Television was not yet available in Australia. There were promises that it would be here **in time for the Olympics in Melbourne in 1956**, so the argy-bargy about the details was starting. **It had been decided** that it would not be a fully government-controlled system (as in Britain), nor would it be handed over to private enterprise (as in America). **It would be the hybrid system** that we have now grown familiar with.

NOVEMBER NEWS ITEMS

A horse won the Melbourne Cup, once again. It had a name, but I forget it. It was brownish I think, if that helps. The man who drove it was wearing strange clothes, including a funny cap, and a bright-coloured shirt. If he had gone off the paddock, he would have **been punched-up by poofter-bashers, who were sadly a current blot on the landscape.**

Madame Ollier, accused by the Petrovs of leaking information to the Russians, told a French Court that she had indeed done that. She explained that everything she had said **was common knowledge and had been in the routine sections of the daily newspapers**. Her comments were checked, and found to be true. As a result, the French Foreign Office has decided that **no blame can be attached to her**.

The Waterside Workers' Federation was insisting that **workers must join the union** before they could get a job on the wharves. The Federal Government **was bringing down legislation that would make this insistence illegal**. A nation-wide strike had held up loading at all Oz ports for a week....

November 12th. The Menzies Government was now proposing **emergency legislation** that would put troops on the wharves, freeze the WWF funds, use the Crimes Act against persons who encouraged strikes, and deregister workers who continued to strike. **These were tough measures indeed....**

The **ship-owners were determined that it was they who should have control over who works for them**, and not the union.

The Federal Government **plans to introduce FM radio** to Australia next year.

The **US Atomic Energy Commission** said that it is not planning any **H-Bomb tests in the Antarctic**.

November 16th. The WWF strike collapsed after an overwhelming vote by the rank and file **to return to work**. It was reminiscent of **the miners' strike in 1949**, when the Government threatened similar intervention. These two strikes brought home to the strikers that **when the Government is ready to play all of its cards**, including the Crimes Act, it can shut down a strike immediately, and the strikers can't win....

The back-down by the WWF put **a dent in the Unions' plans for compulsory unionism.** After all, if the ship-owners could pick their own employees, couldn't every employer?

The Pom cricket team were here, and the knives were well and truly out. The First Test was coming up, and the Oz team was selected last night....

Do you remember Ron Archer, Richie Benaud, Alan Davidson, Les Favell, Neil Harvey, Grahame Hole, Ian Johnson (Captain), Bill Johnston, Ray Lindwall, Gil Langley, Keith Miller, and Arthur Morris. **They were heroes to me**.

THE UBIQUITOUS DR EVATT

In four consecutive days, the newspapers displayed blaring headlines that told a story about how Evatt was cornered by members of the Labor Party for his conduct, and how he escaped discipline. But they show how his antics had split the party, and how close he was to being sacked from the leadership. Most observers at the time said that the only reason he survived in that final vote was because **his heir apparent, Arthur Calwell, was even more of a risk than he was.**

Evatt was also under attack because he had accused the Catholic Action faction of the Party of being disloyal to him and trying to effect his downfall. The Action Group said Evatt was always espousing the spirit of free speech within the Party, but when they exercised it, he accused them of disloyalty. It was all skulduggery, and no one was innocent. But it had **Evatt in the headlines a few more times, and he did not need that**.

By the end of October and into November, **the Royal Commission had presented its interim report**. It concluded that the infamous Document J had been written by a Sydney journalist, Robert Lockwood, and was typed in the Soviet Embassy in Canberra in May that year. "So what?" was the obvious comment. It was only an accusation, with little likelihood of its truth being proved. In any case, the event was hardly very serious in a much bigger world of real spying.

The report cleared the three officers of any misconduct. Then it went on to say that the charges that the Petrov affair was a conspiracy to injure Evatt and the Labor Party "**turned**

out to be fantastic and wholly unsupported by any credible evidence. The conspiracy theory was entirely disproved." In a lengthy document, the Commissioners **discredited the actions of Evatt throughout.**

That, you might think, was that. Evatt had at last been silenced, perhaps you might guess. After all, a Royal Commission had sacked him, his own Party was splitting over his behaviour, and the interim report has said the charges he had laid were fantastic. Surely, you would think, enough is enough.

You would be wrong. Evatt was out the same day saying that the Commission had exercised "scandalous discrimination." And so on. But I warn you. Apart from his verbosity, I have yet to bring you Evatt's ultimate folly. I hope he manages to make this before the end of the year, otherwise you might miss out and die wondering.

LATE CLOSING OF PUBS IN NSW?

People were concerned about this issue. Some of them wanted permanent closure of pubs, others said six o'clock was bad enough but that ten would be much worse. Advocates for family life were adamant that drunken men were a menace, and wanted limitations placed on all men. The serious drinkers wanted late closing because that gave them more time to get drunk, assuming they needed it. The publicans wanted more profits and so did the breweries, so you can guess what they opted for. Somewhere in there were the bulk of the population who would have liked to have the occasional moderate drink without the swill, who wanted to have some wine with their meals on their night-outs, and a game of darts in a pub at night with people who were not drunk. At the moment, there was no chance of any of this.

So, the referendum was a hot issue. The breweries and the Churches put out a great deal of propaganda, and canvassed the matter from every possible angle. I have included some of the better Letters below, but have chosen some that do not push the morality side nor the family suffering side.

Letters, F J O'Brien. The Archbishop of Sydney, Dr Mowll, made a Christian and statesmanlike utterance in his presidential charge to Synod when he advocated a vote for the retention of 6pm closing of hotels.

He spoke not as a narrow partisan but as a community leader who saw the dangers that would flow from further facilities being granted to the liquor trade before it had proven itself worthy of such a trust.

It is true that with the leisurely drinking that is possible on Saturday afternoons far too many men imbibe in a hoggish manner and become a menace to themselves, their families and the public generally. It is a statistical fact that this is the worst day for fatal road accidents of any in the week.

I can see no other result in the granting of a later hotel hour than the mere extension of the "swill" from 6pm to 10pm. This has happened in Queensland and would be inevitable here while the trade is under its present form of conduct and control.

Letters, F E Starley. In fact, the majority in New South Wales sincerely desire greatly improved drinking conditions and the moral cowardice displayed by the State Government in sheltering behind a meaningless referendum is only deserving of contempt.

If the more pleasant features of the English "pub" are to be made available to us here the following steps are essential and must be enforced where possible by suitable legislation:-

The alcoholic content of beer must be halved for at least three years.

The Police Force must be doubled and the "beat" system introduced to assure the public of protection against molestation by drunks.

The number of licensed premises in the metropolitan area must be doubled in the next four years to ensure competitive incentive for the provision of amenities above minimum standards.

The new licences must be granted to interests other than the two main breweries now operating.

The establishment of at least three more breweries in this State must be encouraged. There is little wrong with the "tied house" system but, remember, total power corrupts.

A publican must become liable to forfeit his licence for serving liquor to a person obviously already inebriated; consistent offence against this commonsense rule should be sternly dealt with as an outrage against common decency.

Public hotels must be closed every day between 2.30pm and 6pm. This is of the utmost importance as the habit of drinking large quantities of beer on an empty stomach is a deplorable one. Let a man go home and have his evening meal; after that he will drink less and what he drinks will have less effect on him.

The people of this State will be wise to insist on the foregoing conditions before voting for a measure which, on its own, can only bring degradation and regret.

Letters, M E Wheaton. Until last year I conducted a small manufacturing business in the metropolitan area of Brisbane. I found that hotels being open till 10pm meant that industrial efficiency was impaired and men were either late or absent from work.

It was quite common to see men leaving hotels after 10pm the worse for liquor and in no fit state to be on the job at 7.30 or 8 o'clock the next morning.

Letters, Barton Addison. During a recent tour of Britain I did not see one instance of drunkenness.

Many inns in rural England are happy meeting places in the evenings for village families. Generally beer is the usual drink – and is drunk under decent conditions and not to excess.

I met many American tourists in England and Scandinavia, and those who had been to Australia were loud in their praises of the natural attractions of this country, but without exception they condemned the accommodation.

Letters, A S Webb. In regard to the "6 o'clock swill," about which so much has been written, no one so far has attempted to show that an extension of drinking hours to 10 o'clock will remedy this abomination.

Most men like a drink at the end of their day's work, and what they need is to be able to have it in moderate comfort. The solution is to provide more hotels.

My life-long experience assures me that in this country the brewers frame conditions to suit themselves, and by some mysterious means the Government always comes to heel.

Letters, C A Gregory. 10 o'clock closing would only mitigate the effects of the present archaic set-up. With altered trading should come a form of limited licence to allow any restaurant to serve beer and wines with all food, as is done everywhere abroad.

I saw in Sydney in the first week of my return more drunkenness than I observed in all the other countries in seven months. The continued concentration of drinking in a relatively few brewery-bossed spots will leave the liquor position deplorably defective, whatever trading hours may be settled on.

Letters, Andy de Leede. At present there are about 105,000 adult **new settlers in NSW**, of whom at least 95 per cent would like to have their say on this matter.

They are not heavy drinkers, but want to be able to go to a comfortable place at night (and on a Sunday) to relax and enjoy themselves, and have a drink as well.

The great majority of them have experienced unrestricted drinking hours under the right conditions, which can bring happiness instead of drunkenness.

Comment. The referendum was held on Saturday November 13th, and we will have to wait a few days until the results are in. It looks like being very close. Mind you, **this outcome is not binding on the Government.** If it wants to, it can go against the majority decision of the voters.

THE SHIRLEY BEIGER CASE

A particularly clever Barrister, Jim Shand, defended Shirley Beiger against the charge of murder. He managed to get an all-male jury, and the fact that she was a very pretty model might have been to her advantage. She was distressed throughout the trial, and the fact that she was close to tears throughout again did not hurt her case.

The evidence called was very much along the lines shown in the extract from her statement of events, and the question came down to whether the jury believed that she had not intended to shoot him, and that is was an accident.

The jury found in her favour, and she was acquitted of a charge of murder, and also the charge of manslaughter. This was a very popular decision with the 200 people who crowded the Court at the time, and they cheered her whole-heartedly.   There were, however, many others who thought a different verdict was called for.

They argued that, **to put it in the worst possible light**, she had left the club, gone home and got a gun, and come back and shot him. They went on to argue that this is murder. They also said that it sent a message that, say, "crimes of passion" were not punishable, no matter how deliberate they were. They recalled that in France such crimes were treated leniently, and deplored the verdict as setting a precedent in Australia.

You will have to use your scant knowledge of the case to make your own judgement, though my last word is that there is no sign that I have seen, that such a precedent has penetrated our system.

THE REFERENDUM

When the count was taken on Monday, the early closers were 790,000 and the late closers were 780,000. But as absentee votes came in, and were tallied, they showed a strong drift towards late closing. After a dramatic week, the late closers were 870,000 and they pipped the others by 5,000.

Still, it was far from a landslide, so State Cabinet took it upon themselves to make a decision.

Then they decided to make changes. This did not surprise a lot of people because it was well known that the political Parties were in the pockets of the breweries, and so too were many of the local members. They came out with a number of measures that made the breweries very happy.

The most intriguing decision was to have the pubs close at 6.30 instead of six. **Then, re-open, and stay open till ten.** Clubs, however, would not have the so-called meal-break. The new regulations also allowed restaurants to sell liquors with meals up till midnight, individual pubs must get formal eating premises, and home deliveries of grog must be introduced. Importantly **hundreds of new licences** would be easily granted to Workers' clubs, to RSLs, and to sporting clubs.

It was a staggering set of changes, and I leave you to guess at what the various interested groups said about them. One thing was certain. By now, the opinion of everyone had hardened, and anything that was said would not change any minds at all. Only experience with the reality would do that.

MORE TALK ABOUT MORALITY

You might think that we have had enough talk about morality and depravity, but you would be wrong. The subject of gambling now came to the fore. It appears that religious forces and clergy were against **the State Lotteries**, and were quite prepared to say so.

Letters, E H Burgmann, Bishopthorpe, Canberra.
In the "Herald," November 19, it is reported that the

Premier has said "the Lottery Office was playing tape-recorded messages telling people that the tickets would be ideal Christmas and New Year gifts."

Could anything more incongruous be imagined?

It is generally accepted that Christmas celebrates the birthday of Jesus Christ. With the spirit and practice of gambling there is nothing in common with the spirit and teaching of Christ.

The two are completely incompatible and cannot be reconciled.

Letters, M H Hungerford. Sections of the Christian churches have for years condemned gambling as immoral. No one seems to have had the courage to call their bluff. May I challenge them to reveal their authority, Scriptural or otherwise, for condemning the practice?

I have at times questioned various churchmen on the subject, and have always received evasive answers. Gambling is as old as the human race. The word "lottery" is a Scriptural term. When did the casting of lots or the drawing of a marble become sin?

Letters, Gordon Powell, St Stephen's Presbyterian Church, Sydney. M Hungerford challenges the Churches to reveal their authority for condemning gambling.

Gambling is the desire to obtain something without giving its equivalent in exchange. This is selfishness, which is contrary to the teaching of Christ, "Do unto others as ye would that they should do to you."

In spite of what Mr Hungerford says, the word "lottery" does not appear in the scriptures. The only time the Christian church cast lots was in the choice of a successor to Judas. This was an attempt to find the will of God. With the coming of the Holy Spirit to guide it, the Church abandoned the casting of lots.

Letters, A J Hemmons. Does the individual in our Christian world really need either Biblical testimony or clerical guidance to know what is good or bad for the morals of the community?

Gambling as it is practiced in Australia is nothing less than demoralising, and in many ways a curse. Thousands of people will almost go hungry so long as they can find money to buy lottery tickets.

Letters, Anti-Gambler. It may be of interest to Mr Hungerford to know that God Himself has set out very clearly the end which any consistent and persistent gambler can expect, in Jeremiah, chapter 17, verse 1:

"As the partridge sitteth on eggs, and hatched them not; so he that getteth riches, and not by right, shall leave them in the midst of his days, and at his end shall be a fool."

Most of us know some of whom this has proved true.

Comment. I am not sure what this last Letter means, but I suggest you heed it – or not, as you choose.

DECEMBER NEWS ITEMS

Mr Justice Herron's comment on juries. "If Lucretia Borgia appeared before some of them, they would not convict her under the Pure Foods Act". **Was this a sly comment on the Shirley Beiger case?** If it is just a cute quote, then why did it appear at the top of the *SMH*'s *Column Eight*?

I don't like to crow, so I won't. I will just mention that **Australia won the First cricket Test at Brisbane** by an innings and 154 runs. I will also barely mention that it was the Brits that we were playing. And that **Len Hutton** scored only 4 and 13. **Not that we still resent his 364 against us just before the war**.

In London, an official Australia House committee has decided that all **Australian food for sale should be identified by a symbol**, such as a "Disney-style **kangaroo** – a warm lovable character." That is where the familiar jumping kangaroo imposed on a map of Australia came from.…

A spokesman said that we needed a gimmick. "He could be featured in posters with **Australian fruit-juice dripping from his jaws, or looking at a big thick Australian steak**."

There were many suggestions floating round about how to **improve drinking conditions**. It was suggested that the **lower age limit on barmaids be reduced to 18**, from the current 21. This was rejected. Another was the suggestion, presented to the Legislative Assembly, that **barmaids should be dressed in black, and aged over**

60. Mr Jordan, the Member for Oxley, said that this would discourage men from lingering in bars.

US Senator Joe McCarthy has been under great criticism from moderate Americans for his brutal attacks on people he ignorantly **labelled as Communists**. In December, he maybe went too far. **He attacked the President as an abettor rather that an opponent of Communism.** Even Republican leaders and newspapers were repelled by this....

The *San Francisco Chronicle* summed up America's position. **"American tradition treats extremists and rabble rousers roughly at the end of the road**. It will happen to the confidently arrogant boor from Wisconsin, McCarthy, and we predict it will happen rather soon. After one last momentary flurry in the streams of American history, **he will sink into oblivion."**

In a last ditch attempt to change State Cabinet's decision on the liquor reforms, **clergymen were bombarding the Papers with Letters**. On December 8th, the "united Christians" organised **a protest march in Sydney, but attracted only 1,500 protesters**. And, I must say, to no avail. The Bill that passed 10 o'clock closing into law was accepted on December 10th, and other measures were well in hand.

A poll carried out by the Hollywood magazine, *Box Office*, found that **the most popular star was June Allison**. She was followed by **Gary Cooper, Jane Wyman and Humphrey Bogart.**

HOLLYWOOD MOVIES FOR 1954

Carmen Jones	Dorothy Dandridge, Harry Belafonte, Pearl Bailey
The Caine Mutiny	Humphrey Bogart, Fred McMurray
The Country Girl	Bing Crosby, Grace Kelly, William Holden
The Barefoot Contessa	Humphrey Bogart, Ava Gardner
River of No Return	Marilyn Monroe, Robert Mitchum
Rear Window	James Stewart, Grace Kelly
A Star is Born	Judy Garland, James Mason
The High and Mighty	John Wayne, Robert Stack
Magnificent Obsession	Jane Wyman, Rock Hudson
On the Waterfront	Marlon Brando, Rod Steiger
The Long, Long Trailer	Lucille Ball, Desi Arnaz
Best Actor	Marlon Brando
Best Actress	Grace Kelly
Best Movie	On the Waterfront

HIT SONGS FROM 1954

Secret Love	Doris Day
Mr Sandman	The Chocolates
Little Things Mean a Lot	Kitty Kallen
Oh! My Pa-Pa	Eddie Fisher
Answer Me, My Love	Nat King Cole
Good-night Sweetheart	McGuire Sisters
If I Give My Heart to You	Doris Day
Chapel in the Moonlight	Kitty Kallen
In the Still of the Night	Five Satins
Melancholy Baby	Gloria Gibbs
Someone to Watch Over Me	Frank Sinatra
Tenderly	Nat King Cole
You'll Never Walk Alone	Roy Hamilton
Sh - Boom	The Crew Cuts
Hey There	Rose Clooney
Little Things Mean a Lot	Kitty Kallen

DR EVATT

Well, here we are in December and the Doc has not committed his final blunder of the Petrov enquiry. But he did eventually do so, so I will delve **into next year's items** to put your enquiring minds at rest. Sadly, though, I must be brief.

The Commission continued on its way, but it was not till late September 1955 that it brought down it final report. In it, it said basically that the Petrovs had magnified the gravity of the spying charges, and that the content of their documents and submission contained material that **any inquisitive journalist could have gleaned.** It also found that there were **no charges to be laid against anyone**, though a few people had been careless. **No national secrets were supplied to the Reds. There had been no conspiracy against Evatt.**

That should have wrapped it up. But that supposes that Dr Evatt had gone to ground. He had not. So, it is now that he commits his last big blunder. In mid-October, **he wrote to Russian Foreign Minister, Molotov, and asked him if the Soviet had any spies in Australia.** Molotov replied that Russia did not. Then, believe it or not, for some reason, Evatt read the letters out on the floor of the House of Reps.

The reaction was one of disbelief. He had written to Molotov and asked if he had spies in Australia? What did he expect him to say? Perhaps if he had spies there, he might name them? What could he hope to gain from such a letter? And, why oh why, publicise it on the floor of the House? These were the immediate questions.

The House remained in complete silence for thirty seconds, and then broke out into laughter. **Both sides of the house erupted similarly**. The urbane Menzies then rose, and presented himself as standing for reason, in the face of an opposition that was lacking in it. It was generally agreed that it was one of his finest impromptu speeches, and Evatt never recovered from the whole incident.

EVATT'S FUTURE

The Labor Party lost the 1955 election badly. Evatt was nearly defeated in the seat of Barton, so he transferred to the safe seat of Hunter for the 1958 election. He was still Leader of the Labor Party, but his conduct was becoming more erratic, and in 1960 he accepted the position of Chief Justice of the NSW Supreme Court. This was widely seen as Labor's way of providing him with a face-saving way of leaving politics.

In 1962 he suffered a nervous breakdown, and was persuaded to retire from the bench. He died in 1964.

Comment. He clearly had a brilliant mind, and he was dedicated to the worthy ideals of the Labor Party. There is no doubt that his judgment got worse as time went on, and that has prompted me to write of him the way I have. If I seem to some people to be laying in the boot, I can only say that I am reporting, as an admirer, truthfully what was obvious from the news at the time. That is, the opinions are not mine, but simply a synthesis of current other-peoples' opinions.

CHRISTMAS 1954

Once again, the delightful season of Christmas is upon us. Whether it feels like a steam-roller or a layer of fairy floss upon you is up to you. For me, it's a mixture. I don't really mind the goodwill that pops up here and there, provided the price tag is not too great. I don't mind the eating and drinking, but it goes on too long. I rather enjoy the period of lassitude in January filled with cricket and tennis, but only if my pet teams win. My family enjoy it a lot, so they can talk their heads off with lost family and friends. Not too bad. I wish though that it would happen every third year. That would be enough.

Still, the fact is that it is here, right now. So, I should help you get your presents together. This year, I am working on good things for the adults.

For the gents, there are these manly presents espoused in a very **flowery** column that you might wonder at, but the goods are oh so very good!

For Father – the Old Store has imported a strong but elegant Malacca walking-stick. English, with the horn ferrule and the silver collar. Eighty-nine and six, please. If that's too much out of your pin-money, he'd appreciate a pair of imported Thurston elastic braces, colourfully decorated with hunting scenes, for thirty-one and six.

The Fiance or boy-friend requires a different approach. If you have no ideas at all, describe him to the Diplomat – height, job, tastes, interests, sports. He may suggest a pair of English travelling slippers, in supple leather, tartan lined, complete with leather case, for forty-three shillings. Or 9ct silver lined cuff-links, in gift box for twenty-seven and six. Or a rayon cocktail jacket for six pounds nineteen and six.

The Boss might be good for a New Year salary rise if you offered him a half-box of white lawn English handkerchiefs, wide-hemmed, for fifteen shillings. And the Office Boy or younger brother would like a gay and exclusive Farmer's necktie. From seven and six.

Any man would be glad to have one of the plastic tie-racks – revolving affairs with triple stud tray – cunningly displayed among the feminine fripperies on the Ground Floor for ladies too shy to shop among the men. Seventeen and six, and a bright smile.

The ladies get an equally handsome choice.

Madam, this is the season when you can step daintily into the Esquirely Sanctuary of the Store for Men without your antiblush salts. On the Ground Floor, among the men's mercery and masculine knick-knacks, you'll find your gift problems pre-solved. And on the Lower Ground Floor, too. Graciously, pertly, coyly, or coquettishly, you can mention your man, means and motives to the Diplomat behind the counter and he'll send you away, cool and qualmless, with The Gift wrapped neatly and gaily as befits the season. And would you care for a sneak preview, madam? Then here are Esquire's seasonal suggestions, distilled from as wide and as manly a range as you'd find between the two poles.

Christmas gift furs. For luxury what gift could equal a precious fur? Yet this Christmas, Paris Furs are making many of their lovely furs within reach of the modest purse. This soft, sleek mink-striped marmot cape stole, with tails, is 23 guineas (in silver blue also). A brown musquash straight stole is only 12 guineas, and there are beautiful watermole stoles and capes from 42 guineas. Also for renovations, remodeling, dyeing and cleaning – Paris Furs.

"Bob" – an ideal gift. So many people have realised what an excellent Christmas gift "Bob" is that there are only about 200 left. So look snappy if you're after one. "Bob" is a stapling and tacking tool with a thousand uses. It's invaluable for making or repairing toys, handbags, slippers, canvas covers, harness, etc., for fixing gauze, posters, labels; for installing wires. It will drive staples and nails in the most awkward corners. In a solid wooden box, with 1,000 stainless staples, it costs 29/6 (plus 2/6 postage), from Domex Trading Co.

A good idea. For that something extra-special to wear for Christmas, why not visit Florence Humphrey's little salon, where, in her unique section of worn-only-once-or-twice quality garments, you may find just the thing you've longed for – at a fraction of its original price. We saw attractive frocks and suits for cocktail and street wear in linen, sea island cotton, silk and crepe... some dainty teenage styles, too. Lovely evening gowns, marked down below cost, are from one Pound. Humphrey's.

18 gifts in one. The handiest little gift you could make to man or woman this Christmas is a pair of Universal pocket tool-scissors, they're much more than that... ingeniously incorporated are buttonhole scissors, tracing wheel, nail file, rule, screwdriver, glass cutter, wire cutter, cigar cutter, pipe vice and nine other useful tools. Made of famous Solingen steel and accompanied by instructions.

THE END OF THE YEAR

Now I must take leave of you. It's been nice having you there, and I hope you visit again soon.

When I look back on the year, there are three matters that stick out for me. **The first is the strikes.** I warned you at the start that I would not make much of them day by day, but that you should be aware that they were a constant feature of everyday life. Well, they lived up to that forecast, and they were a never-ending nuisance to the entire citizenry. Sometimes they were pitched at better working conditions, and higher wages. Sometimes they were ideologically driven by Reds who foolishly thought they could bring down the government by creating havoc. A number of them were sheer abuse of power coupled with capricious perversity.

Whatever the cause, they were a pain in the neck, and it was timely when the government pulled the Crimes Act out of its hat with the WWF, and showed them who the real boss was. This lesson took the wind out of big co-ordinated strikers for quite a while, and though the smaller one-day-at-a-time nigglers kept up their pettiness, the scene became a fair bit better for a time.

The second is the Petrov affair. I have covered that substantially, and all I can say is that the nation's first impression was correct. That was, that there was not much that was worth spying on in Oz, and that the Royal Commission would yield no villains at all. The one big result was the sad discrediting of Doc Evatt, and then his later unhappy decline.

The third is the Shirley Beiger case. This raised the issue of whether juries could be manipulated. Could a good-looking person, male or female, together with a theatrical performance, and together with a brilliant barrister, influence a jury made up entirely of members of the opposite sex, to the extent that a dubious verdict might be obtained? This was a question that continued to be argued in pubs across the nation, and elsewhere for a decade, and beyond.

As I look forward, I happen to know that things seemed pretty good for us. **Internationally**, we were an isolated nation, and we were also happy to be insular. There were plenty of events happening overseas, that ordinary people scarcely bothered about. In Indonesia and west New Guinea, in IndoChina, in China, in Africa, in Europe, nations were struggling to be freed for colonialism or fighting for their just place in the world. The average Australian was blithely unaware of much of this, and went about his business with the knowledge that any conflicts were too far away to be of much bother.

As it turned out, he was right. There were a few bumps ahead, such as the Suez crisis, and all sorts of talk about atomic annihilation, but for us the next major overseas problem came with the Vietnam War in the early Sixties. Too far away to worry about in these happy carefree times.

Within Australia, for the bulk of the population, times were good, very good. I won't go through all the economic indicators, but they all pointed the right way. People were prosperous, they were well paid, they had job security, they were buying their own homes, and their kids were well-fed and happy at good educational institutions. What more could you ask for, especially if you looked at it from an international perspective?

There were some problem areas. For example, the Aborigines, the chronically sick and disabled, the poor, and the down-and-out soon to be called homeless. For some of these, help was slowly coming, and for others, there was as yet no sign that society was ready to provide relief for them. Still, again look internationally, and you can see that our situation was better than almost anywhere else.

So the nation was in good shape. One problem that everyone saw was that our politicians, the people who called the tunes on the nation's activities, were not as good as they might be. Here, **we were working, inevitably, on the premise that they should be better than we were. In reality, they were about the same**, and that was a disappointment. Perhaps we should revise our expectations, and then we might find their actions easier to take.

But having rambled for a few pages, it is time to finish off. I hope that if you were born in this year, you went straight out and registered your birth. That way, you became eligible to share in the sixty plus years of happiness that the country has had since then. If you were not so born, then I expect that you too shared in the wonderful years that this nation has experienced, and can be just as contented as the 1954 babies.

In any case, the next time you contemplate, ask yourself whether there has ever been a nation in history that has had a better run than this nation over the last sixty years. I bet you don't find too many.